I Am Born Again,

Now What?

I Am Born Again,

Now
What?

An Invitation to Grow in Christ

Steven J. Campbell

Books for the Harvest
Farmington, New Mexico

I Am Born Again, Now What?: An Invitation to Grow in Christ

© 2014 by Steven J. Campbell

Authors grant permission for any non-commercial reproduction to promote the Kingdom of God.

All other rights reserved.

Published by:
Books for the Harvest
Farmington, New Mexico
USA

ISBN-13: 978-0692279267

ISBN-10: 0692279261

Second Printing—October 2015

Cover image and design by Alex B. Campbell

Chapter 15—Lovesick by Austin J. Campbell

Acknowledgments

As with all authors, I am the result of the influence of many people. I have been impacted by family, friends, other authors, ministers, and churches. All of these have shaped me as a person and author. Even though I am not able to acknowledge each one, I do want to thank a few people that made this book possible:

Susan, my wife—who encouraged me to write even when I thought I could not. Her influence in my life is beyond measure.

Our eight children—each one of you helped me to understand the love of the Heavenly Father better. I want to give a special thanks to Austin, my son, for writing a chapter in this book, and to my son Alex for designing the cover of this book, and to my daughter Anna for the photograph on the back cover of this book.

Pastor Christie DeWees—I thank you for writing the foreword to this book and for all your encouragement throughout the years.

Finally, I thank all of the unnamed family, friends, authors, ministers, and churches whose influence can be seen in this book.

Contents

Foreword

The Word of God speaks of those who have set their hearts toward God. We see their failures and their victories. Most victorious are those who have answered the spiritual question, "Now What?" There is delight in the answer because there is always more.

I have known the author, Steven Campbell, for several years and his passion for relationship is second to none. Steve writes from his heart not just his head. He takes the opportunity to expand the Word of God. Through personal examples and firsthand experience, he walks the reader to discoveries of the answer to the question that we all ask, even if never spoken from our mouths, "Now What?"

This book is impacting and one that for years to come will carry significance to the reader. This book will serve you and take you on a journey of insight to your deepest heart's desires being answered. When God answers the question in our personal lives, it removes the limits and we step onto a path of purpose. May we journey together on the road of life, but truly live on the path, that while it is narrow, it is wide enough for two . . . you and Jesus side by side.

—*Christie DeWees*
Senior Pastor
World Harvest Center
Farmington, New Mexico
USA

Introduction

If you have been born again, it is because you responded to the greatest invitation of all—to receive Jesus Christ as your personal Savior. Even so, what you experienced in the new birth is only the starting point of God's invitation. Yes, His invitation to you is continuing every day—He wants you! You may ask, "Why does He want me?" "What exactly does that mean?"

It means that He wants you to know and experience His feelings for you—He loves you beyond your wildest imaginations. He wants you to experience the friendship between the two of you that He has planned—which will fulfill your deepest desires. For you were created to be filled with the experiential knowledge of God. You were created to experience His love—His loving concern for you. You are made to enjoy God!

He does not just want to be your Savior; He wants to be your friend. We see this fact as Jesus speaks to the church and gives the great invitation to His born-again people:

> *Look! I stand at the door and knock. If you hear my voice and open the door, I will come in, and we will share a meal together as friends. (Revelation 3:20 NLT)*

He wants intimate fellowship with you. He wants to be your best friend. True friendship is enjoying one

11

another's company and He wants you to enjoy Him as much as He enjoys you.

This book is about growing in Christ so that you may be deeply acquainted with the One who loves you and experience His love in a greater measure. His love is not abstract; it is intensely personal. It is the greatest treasure you will ever find.

In the year it took to write this book, I too have heard the invitation for greater fellowship with my Savior. As you read this book it may seem at times that I fully know what I'm writing about, but this is not completely true. I only know a portion of what I write about concerning God's love for me. However, I do want to know more about His great love for me, as well as, how much He loves everyone. This book has helped me to learn more about Him and His love. I count it a privilege to be able to share it with you.

I pray that this book will also help you to discover more of His great love and that you will grow in Christ and enjoy Him every day. Then as you enjoy Him, others will be drawn to you so that you may share God's love with them.

Growing in Christ is your destiny, sharing Him with others is your purpose.

Growth:

THE

FOUNDATION

For no other foundation can anyone lay than that which is laid, which is Jesus Christ.

1 Corinthians 3:11

Chapter 1

Love

*L*ove is the first need of any newborn. In the best-case scenario, children are conceived in love. We know this is often not the case. Many were not conceived or birthed into a loving family. Furthermore, a father or a mother has abandoned countless ones, and both father and mother have abandoned some. A few have even survived their parents attempted abortion. Even so, the Bible has good news for all those abandoned by their parents: *"When my father and my mother forsake me, then the Lord will take care of me"* (Psalm 27:10). We never have to be afraid of being abandoned by God, *"For He Himself has said, 'I will never leave you nor forsake you'"* (Hebrews 13:5).

Far too many children have had terrible beginnings in their lives. However, that is never the case when you are born again. The first thing you need to know as a born-again Christian is that **love** conceived and birthed you. His love is the sure foundation you can stand firmly upon. His love is the starting point of your life as a Christian. 1 John 4:19 states, *"We love Him because He first loved us."*

The foundation of our whole Christian life is based on this one thing—God's love for us. We know about His love for us by the Scriptures. These Scriptures concerning God's love for us are foundational for our growth in Christ.

> *All who confess that Jesus is the Son of God have God living in them, and they live in God. We know how much God loves us, and we have put our trust in his love. (1 John 4:15–16 NLT)*

Though you may have had your love-trust broken from those that should have loved you, you can trust in God's love. God's love for you is the true foundation you can build your life on. No doubt, it will affect every area of your life. In fact, your *trust* in God's love for you will directly influence all your relationships.

> *This is love: not that we loved God, but that he loved us and sent his Son as an atoning sacrifice for our sins. Dear friends, since God so loved us, we also ought to love one another. (1 John 4:10–11 NIV)*

How we are loved affects how we love others. It is harder for a newborn to grow up and be a loving person if they were not loved first. Even if a person had a loving family, they still must learn to love. We all must learn to love.

The first foundation to build upon as a newborn Christian is God's love for you. For you build your life on God. God is love and His love is not some abstract love. His love is personal. He loves *you!* In fact, His love for you is so great that He held nothing back—He gave His only Son for you!

> *For God so loved the world [you] that He gave His only begotten Son, that whoever believes in Him should not perish but have everlasting life. (John 3:16)*

If He did not spare His own Son because of His great love for you, will He not gladly take care of you? *"He who did not keep back his only Son, but gave him up for us all, will he not with him freely give us all things?"* (Romans 8:32 BBE).

The foundation to build your *whole* life on is God's love for you. This is the starting place every day no matter what you are going through or how much you have grown. For the basis of all your growth is love. There are two applications to this love—love God, love others.

> *Jesus replied, "You must love the LORD your God with all your heart, all your soul, and all your mind." This is the first and greatest commandment. A second is equally important: "Love your neighbor as yourself." (Matthew 22:37–39 NLT)*

These commands are God's greatest invitation to you—to love Him and to love others. God not only commands you to love, He gives you His love so that you can love. He is the One who enables you to keep these two commandments. You can love Him and others out of His love.

Love is about relationship. Loving relationships are the key to growth—first with God, then with others. You will not grow beyond the measure of your relationship you have with God and with others. The more you realize this, the more you will pursue love above all things.

If you want to grow to the very fullness of God's purpose for your life, you must know the depth of Christ's love for you. However, you can only experience this by the power of the Holy Spirit working in you.

> *I pray that from his glorious, unlimited resources he will empower you with inner strength through his Spirit. Then Christ will make his home in your hearts as you trust in him. Your roots will grow down into God's love and keep you strong. And may you have the power to understand, as all God's people should, how wide, how long, how high, and how deep his love is. May you experience the love of Christ, though it is too great to understand fully. Then you will be made complete with all the fullness of life and power that comes from God. (Ephesians 3:16–19 NLT)*

Notice how Paul prayed for us in the above verses. He prayed that God would do the work in us by His Spirit. It takes the power of the Spirit to love as we should. The Spirit accomplishes this in us by revealing to us the love of Christ. Jesus loves us with a love that is greater than we can fully understand with our minds.

Yet, when we experience His love, we gain greater understanding of it. To experience God's love **is** the basic reason we were created.

God wants you to experience His love every day. His daily invitation to you is to know His love more—the width, length, height, and depth of His love for you. He really likes you. Nevertheless, you will not come to a full understanding of this overnight. It will come day by day as you grow in Christ.

Companionship

You grow through your time spent with your loving God. This includes your prayer time, Bible reading, being in His presence (worship), and walking with Him. All of these things will take on a completely new life when you realize you are fellowshipping with love. When you are praying, realize you are communicating with a *loving* God who has great pleasure in giving to you (see Luke 12:32). When you read the Bible, realize you are reading a *love* letter written to you. When in worship, realize God simply wants your *love*. And when you walk with Him throughout the day, realize you are walking with *love*, for God is love.

We also grow through our companionship with others. For God did not create us to live alone, He created us to live in contact with others. Even our enemies are included in this. Yes, our enemies can help us grow. Jesus explains this in the following verses:

> . . . *I'm telling you to love your enemies. Let them bring out the best in you, not the worst. When someone gives you a hard time,*

> *respond with the energies of prayer, for then*
> *you are working out of your true selves, your*
> *God-created selves. . . . If all you do is love*
> *the lovable, do you expect a bonus? Anybody*
> *can do that. If you simply say hello to those*
> *who greet you, do you expect a medal? Any*
> *run-of-the-mill sinner does that.*
>
> *In a word, what I'm saying is, Grow up.*
> *You're kingdom subjects. Now live like it.*
> *Live out your God-created identity. Live*
> *generously and graciously toward others,*
> *the way God lives toward you. (Matthew*
> *5:44–48 TMSG)*

Jesus says that we are to live like God. How do we do this? By beholding Him, for we are created to behold Him and become like Him. The more we behold Him by the Holy Spirit the more we will be like Him.

> *But we all, with unveiled face, beholding as*
> *in a mirror the glory of the Lord, are being*
> *transformed into the same image from glory*
> *to glory, just as by the Spirit of the Lord.*
> *(2 Corinthians 3:18)*

God's greatest glory is His love. By receiving and reflecting His love, we are changed—we grow in Christ. His love is the foundation for our lives that will never fail. Love is not some abstract emotion or idea. Love is the very nature of God. His type of love, which can never fail, is explained in 1 Corinthians 13:

Love suffers long and is kind; love does not envy; love does not parade itself, is not puffed up; does not behave rudely, does not seek its own, is not provoked, thinks no evil; does not rejoice in iniquity, but rejoices in the truth; bears all things, believes all things, hopes all things, endures all things.

Love never fails. (1 Corinthians 13:4–8)

When we are born again, we should express the type of love God has. His definition of love will act as our checklist. Do we love with God's type of love? God makes it easy for us to examine our love by comparing it to the above verses.

The Bible is clear that love is of supreme importance. Without love, it does not matter what you can do or say. You could even grow to have all knowledge, understanding, faith, work miracles, and do all of the right things; but without love your life is still empty as 1 Corinthians 13:2–3 states:

If I had the gift of prophecy, and if I understood all of God's secret plans and possessed all knowledge, and if I had such faith that I could move mountains, but didn't love others, I would be nothing. If I gave everything I have to the poor and even sacrificed my body, I could boast about it; but if I didn't love others, I would have gained nothing. (NLT)

Because love is the superior attribute of God, the Bible has much to say about and it does not go around the issue; it hits it head-on:

> . . . *First we were loved, now we love. He loved us first.*
>
> *If anyone boasts, "I love God," and goes right on hating his brother or sister, thinking nothing of it, he is a liar. If he won't love the person he can see, how can he love the God he can't see? The command we have from Christ is blunt: Loving God includes loving people. You've got to love both. (1 John 4:19–21 TMSG)*

Loving God and loving others is Jesus' central command for born-again believers. However, He did not command us to do something that He did not model for us. Jesus Christ modeled what love is. His life embodied love. God's love shown through Jesus is the love that we build our lives on. He is the foundation for our lives.

Always remember, you have the most powerful force in the universe working for you—love. Nothing is a more powerful force than love. Love is the greatest force ever. It is a proven fact. Just look what took place two thousand years ago—the supreme event in history—God sacrificed His own Son. Nothing but love could compel such an action. The cross proves the ultimate power of love. Because of this, the following words take on new meaning: *God is love!*

This is not just the first chapter of this book; it is the "first chapter" for all of your growing in Jesus. If you do not respond to His invitation to believe, receive, and trust in His love for you through Jesus Christ, your growth will be minimal at best. Furthermore, your growth will be hard with little joy. But when you see how much love and joy He has over you, you will grow fast and your growth will include much joy.

[*Please Note:* I've included a personal prayer that I prayed for myself at the end of each chapter. I invite you to pray each prayer with me as it applies to your life.]

Now What?

Father, I need your help. I want to know and experience your love, your love for me and your love for others. I want love to be the foundation of my life. But I can't change myself; I need your help. Holy Spirit, lead me to a greater understanding of love. Help me to receive the width, length, height, and depth of Christ's love for me so that I may keep the two great commandments—loving You and loving others. I ask for these things in and through Jesus Christ. Amen.

We love Him because
He first loved us.

1 John 4:19

Chapter 2

Grace

wo words have captured the hearts of people throughout the years—*amazing grace*. The song, "Amazing Grace" written by John Newton and first published in 1779, is still one of the best-loved songs of all-time. Why? Because we need grace—amazing grace. There are theological definitions that may help us understand grace, however, amazing grace summed-up in one word can give us a greater understanding. That one word is *Jesus*.

Jesus sums-up grace because He is the full picture of grace. *"The Word became flesh and made his dwelling among us. We have seen his glory, the glory of the One and Only, who came from the Father, full of grace and truth"* (John 1:14 NIV). Jesus is FULL of grace. He is the best definition of grace possible. Even the Scriptures show us the grace of God through the person of Jesus Christ.

Our Savior

Jesus Christ is our savior. He saves us by His grace. Grace is a gift from God through Jesus, which brings salvation to us. *"For the grace of God that brings salvation has appeared to all men"* (Titus 2:11). If you are born again, it is by the grace of God.

Grace is the power of God released to us through Jesus. His grace to us is unmerited. We do not deserve it and can do nothing to earn it. Grace is a gift God gives us through Jesus Christ.

> *But God, who is rich in mercy, because of His great love with which He loved us, even when we were dead in trespasses, made us alive together with Christ (by grace you have been saved) . . . that in the ages to come He might show the exceeding riches of His grace in His kindness toward us in Christ Jesus. For by grace you have been saved through faith, and that not of yourselves; it is the gift of God, not of works, lest anyone should boast. (Ephesians 2:4–9)*

God's grace through Jesus brings glory to Him—now and in all future ages to come.

Suffering

Grace delivered us from the punishment of eternal death that we so deserved. *"For the wages of sin is death, but the gift of God is eternal life in Christ Jesus our Lord"* (Romans 6:23). Through the grace of God, we have eternal life. However, grace does not deliver us from suffering. Actually, the God of all grace allows us to suffer; it is part of His will for us.

> *But may the God of all grace, who called us to His eternal glory by Christ Jesus, after you have suffered a while, perfect, establish, strengthen, and settle you. (1 Peter 5:10)*

We need to realize that a part of God's gift to us is the privilege of suffering on Jesus' behalf. *"For you have been given not only the privilege of trusting in Christ but also the privilege of suffering for him"* (Philippians 1:29 NLT). By knowing this we will not think it strange when we suffer after being born again since not all of life's troubles are taken away after our new birth.

> *Beloved, do not think it strange concerning the fiery trial which is to try you, as though some strange thing happened to you; but rejoice to the extent that you partake of Christ's sufferings, that when His glory is revealed, you may also be glad with exceeding joy. (1 Peter 4:12–13)*

The important thing to know is that God will help you in any suffering you go through if you will simply call out to Him. He sits on a throne of grace. A throne speaks of authority. God has the authority to give out grace. Therefore He tells us to come boldly to Him when we need the help of His grace. *"Let us then approach the throne of grace with confidence, so that we may receive mercy and find grace to help us in our time of need"* (Hebrews 4:16 NIV).

Grace does not keep us from all suffering; it helps us in our times of need. Many have not understood this aspect of grace. The grace of God was upon Jesus, but that did not keep Him from sufferings. The same was true of all of Jesus' disciples in the New Testament as well as all of the saints in the Old Testament. The grace of God does not eliminate our afflictions. Knowing this fact strengthens us.

> ... they strengthened the believers. They encouraged them to continue in the faith, reminding them that we must suffer many hardships to enter the Kingdom of God. (Acts 14:22 NLT)

Another Bible version says:

> ... putting muscle and sinew in the lives of the disciples, urging them to stick with what they had begun to believe and not quit, making it clear to them that it wouldn't be easy: "Anyone signing up for the kingdom of God has to go through plenty of hard times." (Acts 14:22 TMSG)

Knowing that hardships are a part of being a Christian makes life easier. You will not be fighting with thoughts of how you must be missing the true Christian life because you are suffering a hardship. Also, it is common to have friends like in the book of Job that will try to convince you that your sufferings are proof that God is disciplining you. But Job knew that his sufferings were not God's discipline. You also need to know that you are not suffering because of wrongdoing.

If you are suffering for being like Christ, that is a good thing. However, if you are suffering because of un-Christlike conduct, that is not good. Make sure you are suffering because of Christ, not for wrongdoing.

*If you are reproached for the name of Christ,
blessed are you, for the Spirit of glory and of
God rests upon you. On their part He is
blasphemed, but on your part He is glorified.
But let none of you suffer as a murderer, a
thief, an evildoer, or as a busybody in other
people's matters. Yet if anyone suffers as a
Christian, let him not be ashamed, but let
him glorify God in this matter. (1 Peter 4:14–
16)*

A hardship may be simply a door into more of your destiny. Hardships try your faith so that you may grow to the place you lack nothing. That may seem like an overstatement, but that is the power of the testing of your faith through various troubles—trials.

*Consider it pure joy, my brothers, whenever
you face trials of many kinds, because you
know that the testing of your faith develops
perseverance. Perseverance must finish its
work so that you may be mature and
complete, not lacking anything. (James 1:2–
4 NIV)*

If we want to be like Jesus and the disciples throughout history, we must embrace this truth. And not just embrace it, but also embrace it with joy as the above verse states, and as they did in the Bible:

*So you received the message with joy from
the Holy Spirit in spite of the severe suffering
it brought you. In this way, you imitated*

> *both us and the Lord. (1 Thessalonians 1:6*
> *NLT)*

Grace for Grace

A major characteristic of Jesus Christ as our foundation is His grace. He is full of grace and truth—*"And of His fullness we have all received, and grace for grace"* (John 1:16). He gives us grace so He can give us more grace—grace for grace. In other words, He wants us to grow in grace. 2 Peter 3:18 says, *"but grow in the grace and knowledge of our Lord and Savior Jesus Christ."*

Since Jesus is full of grace, the best way to grow in grace is to know Jesus more. 2 Peter 1:2 says, *"May God give you more and more grace and peace as you grow in your knowledge of God and Jesus our Lord"* (NLT).

To grow in the knowledge of God and Jesus implies that we have need of more understanding. It indicates that we are seeking to know Him more—we are teachable. This is a major sign of humility. Humility is to know we need grace and to seek it through Jesus. Pride is to think that we do not continually need more grace. Notice how God reacts to pride and humility in the following verse:

> *But He gives more grace. Therefore He says:*
>
> *"God resists the proud,*
> *But gives grace to the humble." (James 4:6)*

I like to go to the throne of grace at the first part of the day and ask for mercy and grace—for I need help every day. We all need God's grace to humble ourselves.

This will result in more grace so that we can humble ourselves even more. This leads to even more grace. Even so, at times I have thought and acted as if God loves me because of some "goodness" within me. However, Jesus gave an excellent parable on humility that challenges those ideas:

> *Two men went up to the temple to pray, one a Pharisee and the other a tax collector. The Pharisee stood and prayed thus with himself, "God, I thank You that I am not like other men—extortioners, unjust, adulterers, or even as this tax collector. I fast twice a week; I give tithes of all that I possess." And the tax collector, standing afar off, would not so much as raise his eyes to heaven, but beat his breast, saying, "God, be merciful to me a sinner!" I tell you, this man went down to his house justified rather than the other; for everyone who exalts himself will be humbled, and he who humbles himself will be exalted. (Luke 18:10–14)*

We should seek God in humility. Humility attracts the grace of God. Humility and grace are major characteristics of Jesus Christ, our foundation.

Grace Teaches

To grow, we all need to be taught. To recognize this need and to acknowledge it shows humility. God responds to this humbleness with His grace, which allows grace to teach us.

For the grace of God that brings salvation has appeared to all men. It teaches us to say "No" to ungodliness and worldly passions, and to live self-controlled, upright and godly lives in this present age. (Titus 2:11-12 NIV)

Currently there is a large amount of teaching on grace. Some of the teaching is departing from the anchor of Scripture. If the grace you are taught does not teach you to deny ungodliness and worldly passions that "grace" is departing from the sure foundation of Scripture. Any grace that does not teach you to live self-controlled, godly lives is not Biblical grace. True Biblical grace makes you eager to do what God says is right.

Grace teaches you to be like Jesus Christ—your foundation. Grace empowers you to model your life after Jesus Christ. He is your example of what it means to live in the grace of God. He showed you how to live your life under grace. He denied ungodliness and showed self-control.

To this you were called, because Christ suffered for you, leaving you an example, that you should follow in his steps.

"He committed no sin, and no deceit was found in his mouth." (1 Peter 2:22–23 NIV)

Grace leads you to follow the example of Jesus. Grace will do a work in your heart where you will hate evil and love righteousness—just as Jesus did.

But to the Son He says:

". . . You have loved righteousness and

hated lawlessness;
Therefore God, Your God, has anointed
    You
With the oil of gladness more than Your
    companions." (Hebrews 1:8–9)

Any grace that influences you away from Christ's example is not Biblical grace. Scriptural grace leads you to Christ and empowers you to live like Him. Then there will be a joy in your life that is apparent to all.

We stand and grow by the grace of Jesus. One of the worst things that we may do is to receive His grace in vain—for His grace to be unproductive in our life. We need to work with His grace. When we yield to His grace, it teaches us self-control. It teaches us to live like Jesus, who lived holy in body and spirit. God expects the same from us—holiness in our spirit and in our body.

> *I beseech you therefore, brethren, by the mercies of God, that you present your bodies a living sacrifice, holy, acceptable to God, which is your reasonable service. And do not be conformed to this world, but be transformed by the renewing of your mind, that you may prove what is that good and acceptable and perfect will of God.*
>
> *For I say, through the grace given to me, to everyone who is among you, not to think of himself more highly than he ought to think, but to think soberly, as God has dealt to each one a measure of faith. (Romans 12:1–3)*

Resist the pride that hinders His grace from teaching you. Pride is a slap-in-the-face to grace. Do not let pride hinder the work of grace in your life. Pride caused the fall of Lucifer (the devil) from heaven. Pride also played a part in the fall of Adam and Eve into sin. Pride is never your friend; it is an enemy to your growth. Here are a few Scriptures from Proverbs:

> *When pride comes, then comes shame;*
> *But with the humble is wisdom.*
> *(Proverbs 11:2)*
>
> *By pride comes nothing but strife,*
> *But with the well-advised is wisdom.*
> *(Proverbs 13:10)*
>
> *Pride goes before destruction,*
> *And a haughty spirit before a fall.*
> *(Proverbs 16:18)*
>
> *A man's pride will bring him low,*
> *But the humble in spirit will retain honor.*
> *(Proverbs 29:23)*

Grace gives us power to grow in Christlikeness, which is the goal of God's grace. Grace is our necessary companion for growing in Jesus.

God invites us to grow by His grace. When pride tries to hinder grace, ask God for the grace to defeat the pride. Pride is our weakness; grace is our strength.

> *[Jesus] said, "My grace is all you need. My power works best in weakness." So now I am glad to boast about my weaknesses, so that*

the power of Christ can work through me.
(2 Corinthians 12:9 NLT)

His grace is all we need to overcome the weakness of pride. *"Therefore humble yourselves under the mighty hand of God, that He may exalt you in due time, casting all your care upon Him, for He cares for you"* (1 Peter 5:6–7).

Let's accept His invitation, come boldly before the throne of grace, and get the help we need!

Now What?

Father, there is nothing more important than You and Your power in my life. Help me to come daily before Your throne of grace to obtain mercy and grace, since I need Your help every day. I want to overcome the fast-pace of life by racing to your throne of grace.

I want to be Christlike, but I can't without Your help, Your grace. Holy Spirit, help me to humble myself and receive Your grace and to live like Christ. In His name I pray. Amen.

But by the grace of God I am what I am, and His grace toward me was not in vain; but I labored more abundantly than they all, yet not I, but the grace of God which was with me.

1 Corinthians 15:10

Chapter 3

Truth

O ne of the best questions ever asked of Jesus was when Pontius Pilate asked, "What is truth?" For you to grow properly, this key foundational question must be answered. When this question is answered correctly, you can have the faith for your growth.

This question ought to be one of the first things answered for a newborn Christian. If you have not had this question answered for you yet, let's find the answer. Actually, the answer is quite simple but humanity has made it complex through their search for the truth. As a Christian, we look to the One with all wisdom and knowledge—Jesus. He answers this very important question for us:

> *Jesus said to him, "I am the way, the truth, and the life. . . . (John 14:6)*

Jesus is Truth! Jesus equates Himself as *the truth.* Jesus embodies truth. Jesus is full of grace and truth. Therefore, Jesus is the foundation of truth that we build upon.

Let's go back to Pilate's question, "What is truth?" to see in what context he asked the question since there is an important detail in the verse just before his question.

> *"You are a king, then!" said Pilate.*
>
> *Jesus answered, "You are right in saying I am a king. In fact, for this reason I was born, and for this I came into the world, to testify to the truth. Everyone on the side of truth listens to me."*
>
> *"What is truth?" Pilate asked.... (John 18:37–38 NIV)*

We find in these verses an important revelation— Jesus is King! He said that He was born to be the King and came into the world as the King to testify to the truth. As King, He has all authority in heaven and on earth.

> *Jesus came and told his disciples, "I have been given all authority in heaven and on earth." (Matthew 28:18 NLT)*

Only one who has all authority in heaven and on earth can establish truth and give eternal weight to his words. Since Jesus is King and has all authority, He can establish truth, give commandments, and expect obedience. Therefore when we speak, our words need to be connected to the authority of Christ. Otherwise, our words may rightfully be received as simply our opinion. Our opinions are not binding upon anyone—they carry no eternal weight. However, if we speak with Christ's authority—His truth with His heart—our words have eternal weight. This is the underlying reason why men try to stop Christians from speaking in His name—His authority. The early church experienced this several times.

But so that it doesn't go any further, let's
silence them with threats so they won't dare
to use Jesus' name ever again with anyone.

They called them back and warned them that
they were on no account ever again to speak
or teach in the name of Jesus. (Acts 4:17–19
TMSG)

If this sounds all too familiar, it is because we are experiencing the same thing today—a forbidding of using the name of Jesus. Why? Because when we speak in His name, our words are no longer just our opinion. People become responsible for Jesus' words. Then if they reject what we say, they are not rejecting our opinion, they are rejecting Jesus—the Truth.

His name offends people because He has the authority to establish what is right and what is wrong. Additionally, everyone will one day be judged by the truth as established by one man—Jesus Christ.

And he ordered us to preach everywhere and
to testify that Jesus is the one appointed by
God to be the judge of all—the living and the
dead. (Acts 10:42 NLT)

Jesus came into the world to show us what truth is. He *is* the truth and if we are in Him, we will hear His voice. Just as sheep know the voice of their shepherd and follow him, so we follow Jesus—our Great Shepherd. Jesus even calls us His sheep saying, *"My sheep hear My voice, and I know them, and they follow Me"* (John 10:27). We follow Jesus, the True Shepherd.

What is God's voice? God's voice is how He speaks to us. God is a conversationalist, so the question is not if God is communicating, but if we are hearing His communications. In Revelation chapters two and three, Jesus continually says, *"He who has an ear, let him hear what the Spirit says to the churches."* The good news is that when we are born again we have the ability to hear and respond to what the Spirit says (see John 10:27). Now all we need to do is to listen to His voice and follow Him, which leads to our growth in Christ.

How does God speak to us? He speaks in various ways. We were born again because of God speaking to our heart. Speaking to our heart with the inward voice of the Holy Spirit is a normal way God speaks (see John 14:26).

Another most important way God speaks to us by the Holy Spirit is through the Scriptures. The Bible is the major way God speaks to us for teaching us how to live, for correcting our actions or attitudes, and for training us in morality so that we may be equipped for everything He has for us.

> *All Scripture is God-breathed and is useful for teaching, rebuking, correcting and training in righteousness, so that the man of God may be thoroughly equipped for every good work. (2 Timothy 3:16–17 NIV)*

The Bible is the communication of God to us. It is His love letter to us—His invitation to an intimate relationship with Him.

Milk of the Word

For those that have just recently been born again, you really need all the help you can get, just as a newborn baby needs someone to help them. So what is the basic need of a newborn? Food is the basic need of every newborn if they are to grow. As a newborn Christian, you too need food to live and grow. What is your food now that you are born again? God tells us in 1 Peter 2:2: *"as newborn babes, desire the pure milk of the word, that you may grow thereby."*

The first basic thing you need for growth is God's word. Without His word, you will not properly grow. However, a newborn also needs affection to mature correctly. If the newborn is force fed and not fed in love, then they will become fussy and angry. So it is with a newborn Christian. When they are force fed and not fed in love, they will become angry and disillusioned. They will feel like they are a bother, not worthy to be fed. God does not force-feed us; He feeds us in love. Too many try to force-feed the word of God to others. *"Instead, speaking the truth in love, we will in all things grow up into him who is the Head, that is, Christ"* (Ephesians 4:15 NIV).

Feeding us *in love* enables us to grow into Christ—who is love. Force-feeding distracts us from the truth that Jesus is love. Force-feeding teaches us that truth is not love, which is the devil's lie. Truth is love and should not be force-fed. Speak the truth in love.

Even Jesus, the Head of the church and Truth personified, does not force His church to hear Him (the Truth). But He stands at the church's door knocking to see if anyone will hear His voice and open the door to Him (see Revelation 3:20).

God speaks to us in many other ways but it is not in the scope of this book to cover those things. We are simply setting a groundwork of truth for the foundation of your faith. Jesus is your foundation and He *is* the truth. Therefore whatever He speaks is the truth—your foundation. *All* Scripture (the Bible) is from God Himself and therefore truth (see 2 Timothy 3:16). God is truth; He does not lie. *"God is not a man, that he should lie, nor a son of man, that he should change his mind"* (Numbers 23:19 NIV).

Your growth will be very limited unless you know that you can completely trust the Bible—the God-breathed word. Your trust in the One who breathed out the Scriptures is vitally important for your growth. The truth in the Scriptures will help you grow as much as anything will. Yet, the truth will not have its full effect unless you believe it to be true. Jesus, the Truth, said that the Scriptures cannot be broken (see John 10:35). Your faith in the truth of the Bible should never be shaken.

> *The main thing to keep in mind here is that no prophecy of Scripture is a matter of private opinion. And why? Because it's not something concocted in the human heart. Prophecy resulted when the Holy Spirit prompted men and women to speak God's Word. (2 Peter 1:20–21 TMSG)*

Daily Bread

However, Scripture is not the only way God speaks truth. Every word that proceeds from the mouth of God is truth. God speaks by His Holy Spirit to us daily—our daily bread. Jesus let us know that we live by every word that proceeds from God.

> . . . *It takes more than bread to stay alive. It takes a steady stream of words from God's mouth. (Matthew 4:4 TMSG)*

Growth takes a steady stream of truth. The more truth you absorb, the more you grow. Even so, *how* you soak up the truth is of extreme importance—with the head or with the heart. We have all seen truth proclaimed by those whose mind was touched by truth but their hearts were not. That is not a pretty thing. Truth in the head without touching the heart results in pride. Truth spoken in pride is repelling. However, truth proclaimed from the heart is compelling. Life-giving truth comes from the heart. This does not mean that truth is always received or that pride is always rejected. But it is certainly true that pride is more repelling while truth is more compelling.

We are to speak the truth in love. Love comes from the heart; pride comes from the head. Knowledge puffs up, but love builds up (see 1 Corinthians 8:1). When the truth is not given in love, it is not very palatable. It seems tasteless without love. Jesus always spoke the truth in love. Nevertheless, the truth He spoke was not always received, but it was not because of a lack of love. So if someone had a hard time receiving the truth you spoke, examine yourself to see if you spoke in love. Love makes truth attractive, although it may not always be acknowledged as truth.

God wants us to embrace truth on the inside not just outwardly. Jesus had very serious words for those embracing truth only outwardly.

> *Woe to you, scribes and Pharisees, hypocrites! For you are like whitewashed tombs which indeed appear beautiful outwardly, but inside are full of dead men's bones and all uncleanness. Even so you also outwardly appear righteous to men, but inside you are full of hypocrisy and lawlessness. (Matthew 23:27–28)*

Relationships are the key to your growth. Without a proper relationship to God and others, your growth will be severely limited. The guidelines for your relationships are found in the Bible. Let the Bible's truths take hold of your heart and not just your head, then you will have true growth.

> *Behold, You desire truth in the inward*
> *   parts,*
> *And in the hidden part You will make me*
> *   to know wisdom. (Psalm 51:6)*

The more you know the Bible, the more growth potential you have—provided it has touched your heart with the truth. Remember, Jesus is full of grace and truth. Grace needs truth and truth needs grace.

"Your words all add up to the sum total: Truth. . . ." (Psalm 119:160 TMSG). The sum of His word is truth. The more of the Bible you know the better off you will be and the easier it will be for you to understand the truth. *"Do your best to present yourself to God as one approved, a workman who does not need to be ashamed and who correctly handles the word of truth"* (2 Timothy 2:15 NIV).

If you want a great life, nothing can produce a greater life than the word of God—that is the lesson of Genesis chapters two and three. Adam and Eve had a glorious life until they disobeyed the word of God, which resulted in them being removed from the Garden of Eden.

Conclusion to Part One— Growth: THE FOUNDATION

Without a solid foundation, we will not grow properly. God's love is the first aspect of our foundation. That love is revealed and experienced through Jesus. Jesus is the manifestation of God's love. We grow by the love-foundation, which is Jesus Christ.

Grace is the second aspect of our foundation in Jesus. His grace empowers us for growth. Without Him we can do nothing (see John 15:5). Though we are weak, His strength empowers us. His grace is sufficient for us.

Through God's love and grace He gives us His Truth—the third aspect of our foundation. The Truth is totally revealed in Jesus Christ. The Word, Jesus, became flesh and lived with us. The Word is Truth. By knowing and abiding in His word, the truth, we are set free.

> ... *If you abide in My word, you are My disciples indeed. And you shall know the truth, and the truth shall make you free. (John 8:31–32)*

Jesus is the foundation for all growth. The Holy Spirit, the Spirit of truth, leads us into all truth (see John 16:12–13). He teaches us and reminds us of *all* Jesus taught (see John 14:26). Our relationship and fellowship with the Holy Spirit brings us into the truth. The Spirit of truth testifies of Jesus (see John 15:26).

God's desire for all of us is:

> *The amazing grace of the Master, Jesus Christ, the extravagant love of God, the intimate friendship of the Holy Spirit, be with all of you. (2 Corinthians 13:14 TMSG)*

Now What?

Father, I want to be like Jesus, the foundation for my life. I want to be full of grace and truth, speaking the truth in love. I want my heart changed not just my head. Holy Spirit, help me to surrender my opinions to the truth of Your word. I invite You to correct me where I need corrected so that I may grow in Christ daily. Spirit of truth, I need you to permeate my heart so that I may be true to my King, Jesus. It's in His name that I pray these things. Amen.

If the foundations are destroyed,

What can the righteous do?

Psalm 11:3

Growth:

THE

BASICS

Chapter 4

The Challenge

I never knew ... until I knew. My core beliefs challenged. What I thought to be true was confronted by the truth. It was a life-changing breakthrough. What did I find? I discovered that there are two opposing views of what it means to be a Christian. Thus began my challenge: Which view would I embrace? What type of Christian would I become?

Truth Brings Freedom

It was March 15th, 1975, my second semester of college, springtime was in the air and new life was sprouting forth when my life changed forever. The traveling minister had our chapel services for the month of March. He simply preached the word of God. I was never the same as the truth set me free because:

> *... the word of God is alive and powerful. It is sharper than the sharpest two-edged sword, cutting between soul and spirit, between joint and marrow. It exposes our innermost thoughts and desires. (Hebrews 4:12 NLT)*

Now let's back-up to the beginning of this story. I was eighteen and attending a Christian college. Why? Because I was born into a Christian family and was raised to be a good person, therefore I thought I ought to go to a Christian college. Additionally, there was a compelling reason beyond this—my first love, Susan, lived nearby and I did not want to be far from her. (We were married the next year—over thirty-eight years of togetherness now.)

I called myself a Christian because I was raised to be one. I believed in the teachings of Christianity. I was a moral person. I did not cuss, drink, or smoke. I tried to keep the Ten Commandments. I went to church and Sunday School. I even prayed at times. From my point of view, I was honest, moral, and good compared to my friends. Therefore, I must be a Christian.

Then came that fateful March day in 1975, the traveling minister had my number. Actually, God had His word for me that day. I never knew before that day that good people who believe in Christianity could go to hell. The word of God cut through me like a sword discerning the thoughts of my heart. The minister preached directly out of Philippians chapter 3 and put a deathblow to my confidence in my own efforts at being a good person.

> ...I never get tired of telling you these things, and I do it to safeguard your faith.... We rely on what Christ Jesus has done for us. We put no confidence in human effort, though I could have confidence in my own effort if anyone could. Indeed, if others have reason for confidence in their own efforts, I have even more! (Philippians 3:1–4 NLT)

My eyes were opened. I realized that there are two forms of Christianity. One is Christianity as a traditional religion that trusts in its own works to be saved from sin and hell. The other form of Christianity trusts only in what Jesus has done for us. One has a faith in Christianity as a religion; the other has faith in Christ alone. One believes you must be a good person to go to heaven, the other believes you must have the goodness of Christ imparted into you by the Holy Spirit.

My wife and I experienced this firsthand when she was saved. If you are not familiar with the Christian term *saved*, it means that everyone is on the road to hell unless God *saves* him or her from it through Christ Jesus. For He came to save us from our sins, which saves us from hell. Jesus is the only one who can save us from sin and hell. To say it another way, the only way to be delivered from going to hell is to be saved first from our sins through Christ. Jesus is the *only* way to heaven because He is the only one who can take away our sins. *"Behold! The Lamb of God who takes away the sin of the world!"* (John 1:29). Without Jesus and His death on the cross, there would be no way to heaven.

Jesus directly challenged the common belief that *most* go to heaven and *few* go to hell when He said:

> *You can enter God's Kingdom only through the narrow gate. The highway to hell is broad, and its gate is wide for the many who choose that way. But the gateway to life is very narrow and the road is difficult, and only a few ever find it. (Matthew 7:13–14 NLT)*

Back to the story again—when my wife was first saved and excitedly informed the members of her church, she was shocked and confused by their response. Many of them did not understand why she needed to be saved. The reply she heard to her proclamation of being saved was, "I thought you were a good person."

This opened our eyes further to the fact that many in the churches think that by being good you get to heaven. It is obvious many trust in what they do to save them: going to church, believing in the church, trying to keep the Ten Commandments, trying to be a good person—all the while hoping that their "good deeds" offset their "bad deeds." Yet, Jesus said that it takes more than trying to be a good person to enter heaven.

> *For I say to you, that unless your righteousness exceeds the righteousness of the scribes and Pharisees, you will by no means enter the kingdom of heaven. (Matthew 5:20)*

God did not save any of us because we were good or trying to be a good person. He saved us when we were sinners. We are **only** saved through Christ and *His* good works:

> *But God demonstrates his own love for us in this: While we were still sinners, Christ died for us.*
>
> *Since we have now been justified by his blood, how much more shall we be saved*

*from God's wrath through him! For if, when
we were God's enemies, we were reconciled
to him through the death of his Son, how
much more, having been reconciled, shall we
be saved through his life! (Romans 5:8–10
NIV)*

One type of the Christian religion tries to get you born into the church. The other wants you born into Christ. They are not the same thing. One wants you to become a follower of the church, the other wants you to be a follower of Christ. When you are born into Christ, then you are born into the church.

Relationship

At this time, the most familiar type of Christian to most of the world is the one who identifies with the religion of Christianity. This type of person would call himself or herself a Christian because they believe in some, most, or all of the teachings of Jesus Christ. They may or may not attend a place of worship (church). They believe they have a relationship with God because of their relationship to a religion.

This is the type of Christianity I discarded on March 15th, 1975. I rejected trying to be saved by my own goodness and I received the goodness of Jesus Christ. I decided to trust no longer in my own righteousness, instead, I chose to trust in Jesus' righteousness as my only hope of salvation from sin and hell.

Many believe that when they die they will enter a place called heaven where God lives since that is what the Christian religion teaches. This person believes that by being, or at least trying to be, a "good person" and living a somewhat moral life, God will allow them to enter heaven—because their "good" outweighs their "bad." We often say when someone is ready to die, "They're ready to go home." If their eternal home is heaven, then this may be true. If their eternal home is hell, they are not prepared for that horror!

When you are born again you are not just getting "fire insurance" from hell. You are getting a relationship with God! Obtaining a relationship with God is the main attraction of the gospel. However, some have made salvation from hell the central part of the gospel. Yes, that is part of the gospel (gospel means *good news*), but the main emphasis of this good news is the *relationship* to God that is available through Jesus Christ. God loves you and wants to have an intimate relationship with you—that is the good news—the best news!

Eternal Life Now

A born-again Christian has eternal life **now**. Having eternal life now is the only way to escape the second death—hell.

> *Most assuredly, I say to you, he who hears My word and believes in Him who sent Me has everlasting life, and shall not come into judgment, but has passed from death into life. (John 5:24)*

Jesus said that when we believe, we have everlasting life. At that moment, we pass from death into life. Eternal life starts when you are born again. It is a gift from God. Eternal life is knowing Father God and His Son Jesus.

> *And this is eternal life, that they may know You, the only true God, and Jesus Christ whom You have sent. (John 17:3)*

Eternal life is having relationship with God. If you do not have eternal life now, then you will die twice—a physical death and then an eternal death.

> *The lake of fire is the second death. If anyone's name was not found written in the book of life, he was thrown into the lake of fire. (Revelation 20:14–15 NIV)*

The Embraced One

When I turned to Jesus years ago, I embraced His work on the cross. He is the Son of God who takes away my sin. I cannot cleanse myself apart from His finished work on the cross when He died in my place for my sins. I embraced Jesus as the only way to have eternal life.

> *For God so loved the world that He gave His only begotten Son, that whoever believes in Him should not perish but have everlasting life. (John 3:16)*

Challenges Still

Even though I have embraced Jesus as the source of my righteousness, it still seems too easy to be foolish by trusting in my own human efforts. Indeed, I need reminded daily that it is not about me; it is about Him.

It is about what He has done for me through His Holy Spirit.

> *How foolish can you be? After starting your Christian lives in the Spirit, why are you now trying to become perfect by your own human effort? (Galatians 3:3 NLT)*

I am constantly learning not to be foolish—to not trust in my own human effort.

I told my personal challenge in dealing with the two types of Christianity so that you may examine your own experience. For you want to make sure that you truly belong to Christ.

> *Test yourselves to make sure you are solid in the faith. Don't drift along taking everything for granted. Give yourselves regular checkups. You need firsthand evidence, not mere hearsay, that Jesus Christ is in you. Test it out. If you fail the test, do something about it. (2 Corinthians 13:5 TMSG)*

The First Step

The first step is to make sure you are born again into Christ and not just into Christianity. Why? Because many in the church are not born again. We experienced this fact several years ago. We were members of a rather large church when numerous members realized they were not born again. Through the work of the Holy Spirit, many were convicted of their sin—not believing in Jesus for their salvation. Our not believing in Jesus is the sin that the Holy Spirit convicts us of.

And when He [the Holy Spirit] has come, He will convict the world of sin . . . of sin, because they do not believe in Me . . . (John 16:8–9)

The conviction of the Holy Spirit was so strong in those days that I was afraid to go to church and afraid not to go. I would open the doors to the church long before anyone arrived. I would be trembling knowing God's word was going to be coming forth in a few hours. I would go from corner to corner of the building burying my face in each corner crying out for His word to come forth by the Spirit. I would tremble when I thought about His word being preached under the power of the Holy Spirit.

For sure, I was not the only one trembling at God's word. Many in the church began to experience Isaiah 66:2 as we humbled ourselves.

. . . I will bless those who have humble and contrite hearts, who tremble at my word. (Isaiah 66:2 NLT)

As we sat in our seats, the minister would proclaim the word of God and we would tremble. What was the message that caused us to tremble at God's word? It was that we are not saved by our membership in a Bible-believing-church, or by our good works, or by a moral life—but only by Jesus' work.

The Spirit anointed the word of God exposing the thoughts and intents of our hearts. God's word caused us to examine ourselves to see if we were trusting in Jesus' work on our behalf, or if we were trusting in our own efforts. Many were surprised to learn that their trust was not actually in Jesus. Their faith was turned from their "good works" to His great work on the cross. Even those of us who knew that we were born again through trusting in Jesus' work found ourselves repenting for not fully trusting in Him as we should have.

Questions like this challenged us: "Have you experienced the change of lordship in your life?" "Has there been a time where you surrendered the control of your life to Jesus?" These are also excellent questions for you to ask. Who is the lord of your life?

It is essential that you *proclaim* that Jesus is Lord to be saved, but that confession must come from your heart and not just your head.

> *Because, if you say with your mouth that Jesus is Lord, and have faith in your heart that God has made him come back from the dead, you will have salvation:*
>
> *For with the heart man has faith to get righteousness, and with the mouth he says that Jesus is Lord to get salvation. (Romans 10:9–10 BBE)*

When you say, "Jesus is Lord," what does that mean? It means you are saying that Jesus is the One with authority over your life. You are confessing Him as your Master, your Lord. The change to His lordship will alter your life. However, everyone's change will be unique. Some will have radical change and some will have less visible change. Some will go from acting like "the devil" to acting like Jesus, while others will go from acting like "a Christian" to *being* a Christian—going from being a "good" person to being a godly person.

"Good people" do not go to heaven. God's people go to heaven—those in Christ. Only those who have Christ living in them will experience heaven. Of course, if Jesus is Lord of your life, you will be a good person doing good things. Even so, it is Christ being in you that is your hope of glory (see Colossians 1:27).

Ultimate Challenge

Our freewill is our ultimate challenge. A major weakness of human freewill is trying to make ourselves like God. That was the initial temptation that humankind fell into. Adam and Eve were already like God because of what He had done—made them in His image. The devil tempted them to make themselves like God through doing things their own way instead of trusting in what God had already done.

God planted two special trees in the Garden of Eden. One was the tree of life, which represented God's provision—Jesus. The other tree was the tree of knowledge of good and evil, which represented trying to be like God through human effort—religion. Man was not created for the knowledge of good and evil—dos and don'ts. Man was created to behold and partake of the tree of life. Man was created for Jesus (see Colossians 1:16).

In God is *all* the wisdom and knowledge we need as Colossians 2:3 states, *"in whom are hidden all the treasures of wisdom and knowledge."* We need to seek God, not the knowledge of good and evil.

Which tree will you choose? Will it be the tree of knowledge of good and evil, dos and don'ts—religion? Or, will it be the tree of life—Jesus, in whom is hidden all wisdom and knowledge? The choice of trees was the ultimate challenge for humanity's freewill in the Garden of Eden. This is still our challenge today.

God wants us to partake of the tree of life and enter into His rest. He wants us to rest in His finished work. Because of this, He blessed the day that He rested more than the days He worked.

> *And on the seventh day God ended His work which He had done, and He rested on the seventh day from all His work which He had done. Then God blessed the seventh day and sanctified it, because in it He rested from all His work which God had created and made. (Genesis 2:2–3)*

Resting in God's work is our calling and our greatest challenge. To rest in God is to rest in what He has already done for us. We are already in His image when we are born again (2 Corinthians 5:17). The problem is that we are created by the Creator with an abundance of creativity. Therefore, the challenge is: "Are we going to submit our creativity to His authority?"

> *For we are His workmanship, created in Christ Jesus for good works, which God prepared beforehand that we should walk in them. (Ephesians 2:10)*

God has given us many wonderful things to do, but our creativity must be subjected to His will. Jesus, our example, overcame the temptation to use His creativity outside of the will of God:

> *Now when the tempter came to Him, he said, "If You are the Son of God, command that these stones become bread."*
>
> *But He answered and said, "It is written, 'Man shall not live by bread alone, but by every word that proceeds from the mouth of God.'" (Matthew 4:3–4)*

If you want to grow, you need to come face to face with the challenge of doing things your way or God's way. You have the invitation to grow by living in His word—His will. Submit to God's way and win the challenge!

Now What?

Father, I need the help of Your Holy Spirit to overcome my tendency to trust in my own efforts to be pleasing to You. Holy Spirit, help me to remember I am already pleasing to You because of what Jesus did for me. Help me to see clearly the daily choices before me, and help me to choose life—the life in Jesus.

Father, forgive me for trusting in myself when I should have trusted in You. Even though I have failed many times, I still want to trust *only* in You.

Thank You for saving me by Your blood—the blood of Jesus. Thank You Jesus for suffering for me. In Your name I pray. Amen.

And this is the secret: Christ lives in you. This gives you assurance of sharing his glory.

Colossians 1:27 NLT

Chapter 5

The Answer

*T*he greatest work you can do is to cease from your works. For your work is to rely on His finished work. His work on your behalf was finished on the cross. If you want to go on to maturity in Christ, this is where you start—at the cross. This is the doorway into maturity. However, it is a great challenge to cease working and enter into His rest.

Even so, God invites us to cease from our labors and enter into His completed labor. If we do not respond to His invitation to enter His rest, according to the following Scripture, we will fall.

> *God's promise of entering his rest still stands, so we ought to tremble with fear that some of you might fail to experience it. For this good news—that God has prepared this rest—has been announced to us just as it was to them. But it did them no good because they didn't share the faith of those who listened to God. For only we who believe can enter his rest. . . .*
>
> *So God's rest is there for people to enter, but those who first heard this good news failed to enter because they disobeyed God. So God*

> *set another time for entering his rest, and that time is today. . . .*
>
> *"Today when you hear his voice, don't harden your hearts."*
>
> *. . . So there is a special rest still waiting for the people of God. For all who have entered into God's rest have rested from their labors, just as God did after creating the world. So let us do our best to enter that rest. But if we disobey God, as the people of Israel did, we will fall. (Hebrews 4:1–11 NLT)*

Christianity is not trusting in your good works to please God. Faith in your own works, your own effort, is not what pleases God. What pleases God is your faith in His works—your faith in Him. Without that faith, you can never please God.

> *But without faith it is impossible to please Him, for he who comes to God must believe that He is, and that He is a rewarder of those who diligently seek Him. (Hebrews 11:6)*

We are to seek God diligently. That is where we will find rest. True rest is God Himself. If we want to grow, we will let God do the work in us. We will rest in His work in our life. The more we try to fix ourselves, the more frustrated we will be. But when we let God do the work in us, we will be at peace (rest) knowing that we are His masterpiece. *"For we are God's masterpiece. He has created us anew in Christ Jesus, so we can do the*

good things he planned for us long ago" (Ephesians
2:10 NLT).

God is the author **and finisher** of our faith. It was
His idea to save us. He will complete His work in us. We
need to have faith in Him. We need to lay aside
everything that would hinder us from keeping our eyes
on Jesus.

> *. . . let us lay aside every weight, and the sin
> which so easily ensnares us, and let us run
> with endurance the race that is set before us,
> looking unto Jesus, the author and finisher of
> our faith . . . (Hebrews 12:1–2)*

We know that we have things to do in this life, so
entering His rest does not mean that we will not do
things. It means that we allow Him to work through us.
He produces our works as we yield to Him. We will have
fruitful lives because we abide (dwell, remain) in Jesus.

> *Abide in Me, and I in you. As the branch
> cannot bear fruit of itself, unless it abides in
> the vine, neither can you, unless you abide in
> Me.*
>
> *I am the vine, you are the branches. He who
> abides in Me, and I in him, bears much fruit;
> for without Me you can do nothing. (John
> 15:4–5)*

Christ, the Foundation

There is only one foundation to build on (see
1 Corinthians 3:11). Jesus is our only foundation. He is

our sure foundation, our eternal foundation. He is the foundation we must build on. If we do not start here, we will eventually end up falling. Our foundation is trusting in the work of Jesus and not our own works. This is the **first** elementary principle to build our life on.

> *Therefore, leaving the discussion of the elementary principles of Christ, let us go on to perfection, not laying again the foundation of repentance from dead works and of faith toward God. (Hebrews 6:1)*

Hebrews 6 speaks about us leaving the discussion of the basic principles of Christ. However, before we leave emphasizing the basics of our foundation in Christ, we need to have those elementary principles firmly established in our lives. The first basic foundational principle of Christ is *"repentance from dead works **and** faith toward God."* These two things go hand-in-hand. Do not try to do one without the other; it will not work. Turn to God and away from dead works.

"Repentance from dead works" is when you turn your back on trusting in your own efforts, your own good deeds, and your own power to change your life. Instead, you turn to *"faith toward God."* You are trusting in His work in you and for you. He is the One who can change your heart. Stop trying to change yourself. Keep focusing on God; He is the Great-Heart-Changer. Let God do what He is best at—drawing you to Himself and changing your heart.

Before you can fully embrace this basic principle of Christ, you need His cleansing. You must have your conscience cleansed from feeling as if you have to perform to be pleasing to God. Without this cleansing, you will not be able to serve the living God—to grow in Christ.

> *How much more shall the blood of Christ, who through the eternal Spirit offered Himself without spot to God, cleanse your conscience from dead works to serve the living God? (Hebrews 9:14)*

Since this is such a vital truth to grasp and is contrary to many people's concept of Christianity, we want to show this truth again from another translation:

> *Think how much more the blood of Christ cleans up our whole lives, inside and out. Through the Spirit, Christ offered himself as an unblemished sacrifice, freeing us from all those dead-end efforts to make ourselves respectable, so that we can live all out for God. (Hebrews 9:14–15 TMSG)*

If you want to live *"all out for God,"* you must have your conscience free from self-effort to please God. You are already pleasing to God because of what Jesus did for you on the cross. Stop striving for what you already have in Christ. Allow His sacrificial blood, shed for you, to cleanse your conscience. Do not give into the human tendency to *focus* inwardly on your own self, but **focus on Jesus** and His ability to change you. Too much introspection (inward focus) will hinder you from living *"all out for God."*

God has great pleasure in us when we are in His Son Jesus Christ (born again). God brought us to Himself through Jesus. He sees us as holy and without fault when we are in Christ. Truly, you are right with God through Christ.

> *Even before he made the world, God loved us and chose us in Christ to be holy and without fault in his eyes. God decided in advance to adopt us into his own family by bringing us to himself through Jesus Christ. This is what he wanted to do, and it gave him great pleasure. (Ephesians 1:4–5 NLT)*

We can go into the very presence of the most holy God because of our faith in Jesus. We can be confident in what we are in Him. *"Because of Christ and our faith in him, we can now come boldly and confidently into God's presence"* (Ephesians 3:12 NLT).

To experience the presence of God is what we were created for. Nothing can satisfy us more than His presence. In His presence is fullness of joy (see Psalm 16:11). But there is only one way to come boldly into God's presence. It is through Jesus and our faith in Him.

The Bible is always encouraging us to not trust in ourselves, but to trust in God. In fact, the Scriptures forcefully argue for us to give up self-righteousness and receive God's righteousness.

> *I don't mind repeating what I have written in earlier letters, and I hope you don't mind hearing it again. Better safe than sorry—so here goes.*

I didn't want some petty, inferior brand of righteousness that comes from keeping a list of rules when I could get the robust kind that comes from trusting Christ—God's righteousness.

I gave up all that inferior stuff so I could know Christ personally, experience his resurrection power, be a partner in his suffering, and go all the way with him to death itself. (Philippians 3:1, 9–10 TMSG)

We cannot go all the way with Jesus unless we are willing to receive His righteousness, giving up our self-righteousness. The first step in maturity is receiving and walking in what Jesus already did for us. We are right with God **in** Christ. *"We are made right with God by placing our faith in Jesus Christ. And this is true for everyone who believes, no matter who we are"* (Romans 3:22 NLT).

It is so foolish to trust in our own efforts to please God. Furthermore, the Scriptures show that religion is foolishness unless it is based upon what God does for us. I think of religion as humanity's attempt to meet God's standards. In contrast, true Christianity is God meeting His own standards in Christ and then imparting those standards through Christ into us.

We are the product of His workmanship; we are His masterpiece. He is the Great Artist. Why would we presume to make a "better painting" through our own work? Who would presume to add their work to Leonardo da Vinci's masterpiece, the *Mona Lisa?* How much more prideful it is to think we can produce a better masterpiece of our lives than God can.

> *For we are God's masterpiece. He has created us anew in Christ Jesus, so we can do the good things he planned for us long ago. (Ephesians 2:10 NLT)*

We are created anew in Christ by our faith and not our good deeds, so we can produce good works. Our good works are to come out of our relationship with Christ, just as Jesus' works came out of His relationship with His Father.

> *. . . Most assuredly, I say to you, the Son can do nothing of Himself, but what He sees the Father do; for whatever He does, the Son also does in like manner. (John 5:19)*

Jesus set the example for us of having our good deeds come out of our relationship with God. It is out of our relationship with Him that we are able to bear good fruit. Just as a tree needs to be rooted and grounded in good soil to produce good fruit, so we need to be rooted in Jesus to produce good things. Without His life flowing through us, we will not bear good fruit.

Jesus is the author and finisher of your faith. He chose to save you and start your life in Christ. It took His power to save you through your faith in Him. In the same way, it will be His power and your faith in Him that will complete your growth in Christ. He is the **author and finisher** of *your* faith.

The following Scripture is very straightforward in how God views trusting in our own efforts to finish what He started:

> . . . *Did someone put a hex on you? Have you taken leave of your senses? Something crazy has happened, for it's obvious that you no longer have the crucified Jesus in clear focus in your lives. His sacrifice on the Cross was certainly set before you clearly enough.*

> *Let me put this question to you: How did your new life begin? Was it by working your heads off to please God? Or was it by responding to God's Message to you? Are you going to continue this craziness? For only crazy people would think they could complete by their own efforts what was begun by God. If you weren't smart enough or strong enough to begin it, how do you suppose you could perfect it? Did you go through this whole painful learning process for nothing? It is not yet a total loss, but it certainly will be if you keep this up!*

> *Answer this question: Does the God who lavishly provides you with his own presence, his Holy Spirit, working things in your lives you could never do for yourselves, does he do these things because of your strenuous moral striving or because you trust him to do them in you? . . . And that means that anyone who tries to live by his own effort, independent of*

*God, is doomed to failure. (Galatians 3:1–10
TMSG)*

Our confidence is in God and His workmanship in us. He will complete the work He has started in us. The Scripture states, *"being confident of this, that he who began a good work in you will carry it on to completion until the day of Christ Jesus"* (Philippians 1:6 NIV).

We are close to *"the day of Christ Jesus."* Because of this, these are important days to enter into God's rest—obedience. Obedience is yielding to God's work in us. Disobedience is pride, thinking our plans are better for us than God's will for us. Yield to God and watch how fast we can grow, for in Christ we have extraordinary growth potential.

When we are in Christ, we are new. We are not the same person. We are no longer looking to ourselves as the answer to our questions, but we have a completely new outlook on life because God has made us a new person.

> *Therefore, if anyone is in Christ, he is a new creation; old things have passed away; behold, all things have become new. (2 Corinthians 5:17)*

What would it look like to cease from our own works and to enter God's rest as this newly created person? The next chapter will show us what this looks like.

Now What?

Father, I want to trust totally in Your work in my life and not in my efforts. I believe that You are the rest for my soul. Help me to always seek You and not the things of this world.

Father, I see Your work in my life up to this point, and I thank You for it. I know that You will finish the work You have started in me.

Holy Spirit, continue to cleanse my conscience from feeling I have to perform to be pleasing to You. For I know I am pleasing to You when I believe what You have done for me. I want to live all out for God; so, Holy Spirit, continue to free me from my useless efforts to make myself respectable. Only You can change my heart. I am Your masterpiece. I choose to trust in Your work through Christ Jesus. It's through Him I pray this. Amen.

For he who has entered His rest has himself also ceased from his works as God did from His.

Hebrews 4:10

Chapter 6

The Example

C hildren learn by observation. As a child of God, you will grow by *seeing* how Jesus lived when He was on the earth. In addition, you will learn and grow by seeing "Jesus" in other people who follow Him. In other words, you will grow by observing the life of Christ—including seeing His life in others.

Little children want to understand about the things they *see*. They grow fast in the things they observe because they are teachable. This is one of the greatest characteristics of humility—being teachable. If we will be like a little child when it comes to following Jesus, we will be teachable and grow fast. In fact, Jesus says that we will never enter the kingdom of heaven unless we become like little children.

> *And he [Jesus] said: "I tell you the truth, unless you change and become like little children, you will never enter the kingdom of heaven. Therefore, whoever humbles himself like this child is the greatest in the kingdom of heaven." (Matthew 18:3–4 NIV)*

God wants us to be humble—teachable like little children. He wants us to change by observing how He lived life. For God did not just tell us how we ought to live, He showed us. He gave us the best example to follow—His Son, Jesus Christ. Jesus lived His life on earth as the Son of Man while being the Son of God. He lived as a *man* upon the earth so we could follow His example. That is, He came as the Son of God but *lived* as the Son of Man. He is our supreme example of how to live life.

God also gave us many examples in Scripture and in contemporary history of how to live the Christian life. Without a doubt, God wants us all to be examples of how to live. Even a newborn Christian can be an example of how to live because they are a new creation in Christ. Their heart is to follow Jesus even if some areas of their life still need changing (of course, this is true for all of us). No matter how long we have been a Christian, don't we want to be able to say, *"Imitate me, just as I also imitate Christ"?* (1 Corinthians 11:1).

The Way

Jesus calls Himself the Way in John 14:6. This statement has more meaning than what we may have understood. The word *way* carries the meaning of: road, path, the way to travel. Jesus is the only way to get to God the Father. *"Jesus said to him, 'I am the way, the truth, and the life. No one comes to the Father except through Me'"* (John 14:6).

Jesus is the Way—the road, the path, the way to travel. That is why Jesus said, *"Follow Me."* We are to be imitators of Christ. We are to walk as He walked—to live as He lived. He set the path for us to walk, the road map for us to follow. He showed us the way of travel. He is the Way in which we should go. Follow Him!

Jesus demonstrated for us how to live pleasing to God. He showed us that we please God by being what God made us to be. He pleased God before He ever was in "full-time ministry." He totally pleased God as a carpenter!

You need to live as He did—free from trying to please God through your own works. Your full-time ministry is whatever you are called to do. It will be in one of the seven-fold aspects of society. It may be in the sphere of: family, education, economy, religion, government, media, or the arts and entertainment. Wherever God has called you to function, serve God there.

Jesus was the freest person ever to live on earth. He was free to do whatever God wanted Him to do. True freedom is not being able to do whatever you want; it is being able to do whatever God wants. Adam and Eve were truly free to do whatever they wanted until they were not able to do what God wanted. When they did not do what God wanted—they ate from the tree of knowledge of good and evil—they lost true freedom. They were free until they disobeyed God. True freedom is only found in obeying God from the heart. It may be a struggle at times, but that only magnifies the obedience—the freedom to obey God.

Since God loves you beyond your wildest imagination, His desires for your life are in your best interest. Yes, He desires the best for you, which is the freedom to be all He created you to be. So whatever He asks of you is for your ultimate good. Therefore it is always foolish to disobey the One who has your best interests in mind. Adam and Eve, as well as countless other examples in the Bible, show us the foolishness of disobeying God.

To walk in freedom is to be devoted to obeying God. *"I will walk in freedom, for I have devoted myself to your commandments"* (Psalm 119:45 NLT). We find this issue explained skillfully in Romans 6:

> *. . . Since we're free in the freedom of God, can we do anything that comes to mind? Hardly. You know well enough from your own experience that there are some acts of so-called freedom that destroy freedom. Offer yourselves to sin, for instance, and it's your last free act. But offer yourselves to the ways of God and the freedom never quits. All your lives you've let sin tell you what to do. But thank God you've started listening to a new master, one whose commands set you free to live openly in his freedom!*
>
> *I'm using this freedom language because it's easy to picture. You can readily recall, can't you, how at one time the more you did just what you felt like doing—not caring about others, not caring about God—the worse your life became and the less freedom you had? And how much different is it now as you live in God's freedom, your lives healed and expansive in holiness?*
>
> *As long as you did what you felt like doing, ignoring God, you didn't have to bother with*

*right thinking or right living, or right
anything for that matter. But do you call
that a free life? What did you get out of it?
Nothing you're proud of now. Where did it
get you? A dead end.*

*But now that you've found you don't have to
listen to sin tell you what to do, and have
discovered the delight of listening to God
telling you, what a surprise! A whole, healed,
put-together life right now, with more and
more of life on the way! (Romans 6:15–22
TMSG)*

Wow! Isn't this what we all want? Without a doubt,
God is inviting us to true freedom—through full
obedience. Jesus lived in total obedience to the Father's
will and was the freest man to ever live. Likewise, we are
only free to the extent of our obedience to God, because
we are created to be in God's image. Therefore, it is
natural for us to be godly—like God. And His
commandments will free us to be all we are created to
be.

Son of God

Jesus came to earth as the Son of God to show us
what God is like. He personified God. He made God real
to everyone, showing us what God is and demonstrating
Him in His life. Jesus knew this is why He came to earth
so He boldly proclaimed, *"He who has seen Me has seen
the Father"* (John 14:9). Jesus' life perfectly reflected
God the Father.

Son of Man

Jesus also came to earth as the Son of Man to show us how a person is to live their life—what a human being is to be like. Yes, Jesus is God, but He lived as a man to demonstrate how we should live. He lived a holy life. This means He lived a life set apart to God. It is shocking to many people that God expects us to live as Jesus did. However, He enables us to live this way by giving us Jesus' example and by sending the Holy Spirit to live in us. We can be partakers of the divine nature and escape the world's corruption by the power of God. We can!

> *His divine power has given us everything we need for life and godliness through our knowledge of him who called us by his own glory and goodness. Through these he has given us his very great and precious promises, so that through them you may participate in the divine nature and escape the corruption in the world caused by evil desires. (2 Peter 1:3–4 NIV)*

Through our believing in all that Jesus has done for us, we can be like Jesus. *"For all the promises of God in Him are Yes, and in Him Amen, to the glory of God through us"* (2 Corinthians 1:20).

Jesus is the answer to what it looks like for a person to live their life trusting in the power of God. Moreover, He wants us to live as He lived, and trust God as He trusted God. God will take care of all our needs. Jesus promised us this when He said, *"But seek first the kingdom of God and His righteousness, and all these things shall be added to you"* (Matthew 6:33).

Jesus fully obeyed God, thus having the greatest life ever lived. He was completely free because He embraced all the will of God for His life. He had more peace than anyone else ever had, and was full of joy like none other. You can have the same righteousness, peace, and joy if you will seek first the kingdom of God as Jesus did. *"For the kingdom of God is . . . righteousness and peace and joy in the Holy Spirit"* (Romans 14:17). This is the divine order for the joy you desire. First, do what God says is right (righteousness) which will lead to peace. Then righteousness and peace leads to joy. This is all accomplished *"in the Holy Spirit."* By following the Holy Spirit, you will walk in righteousness, peace, and joy.

When you follow the Holy Spirit into these things, you will be like a light in the dark. You will stand out as strange, as abnormal. People will ask you, "Where do you get such peace and joy?" They will marvel at your joy saying, "Why are you so happy?" And you will be able to answer: "It is because of Jesus; I follow His example of how to live. I follow the leading of the Holy Spirit of God. I live in obedience to God, which gives me great peace and joy. The joy of the Lord is my strength."

Jesus' joy was to do the will of the Father. Do you want your life to be the happiest possible? Of course you do. The way to be the happiest is to stay in the will of God for your life. Jesus was the happiest person ever because He stayed in the will of God.

It may be shocking for some, but God is the happiest being ever! In His presence is the complete fullness of joy and pleasure. If you want this, simply follow the path of life, the Way of Life—Jesus.

> *You will show me the path of life;*
> *In Your presence is fullness of joy;*
> *At Your right hand are pleasures*
> *forevermore. (Psalm 16:11)*

Jesus is Life. The fullness of life is in Jesus. If you want a full life, it is found in Jesus. He came to give you growth in Him. Growth signifies that something is alive. If growth stops, life stops. Never stop growing in Jesus. You should also know that He came to give you abundant growth. Therefore, don't allow anyone to rob you of your full-growth through Christ.

> *I have come that they may have life, and that*
> *they may have it more abundantly. (John*
> *10:10)*

The Garden

We face the same choice as Adam and Eve had in the Garden of Eden. In the Garden was the choice of the tree of the knowledge of good and evil. This tree causes you to look inward—to look at yourself to see the good and the bad, which causes you to compare yourself to others.

Through self-examination you can easily find problems within, but you cannot fix the problems yourself. Adam and Eve discovered this when they chose the tree of knowledge of good and evil. They examined themselves and found that they were naked, so they tried to fix the situation. But their fig leaves were no real fix; it took God to clothe them. So also, it takes God to repair any wrong in us.

Do you want to know what you are really like so you can "fix" yourself? Or, do you want to know what God is like so you may be like Him? The tree of Life causes you to look outward—to see God—to see yourself from God's perspective. Choose the tree of Life for we are not changed by looking inward but outward. By beholding God, we are changed.

> *But we all, with unveiled face, beholding as in a mirror the glory of the Lord, are being transformed into the same image from glory to glory, just as by the Spirit of the Lord. (2 Corinthians 3:18)*

When we walk as Jesus did, we are changed; we grow. When we walk on the path Jesus is walking, He cleanses us from all sin.

> *But if we walk in the light, God himself being the light, we also experience a shared life with one another, as the sacrificed blood of Jesus, God's Son, purges all our sin. (1 John 1:7 TMSG)*

Keep in mind that when the Scriptures speak of judging ourselves and examining ourselves, this is to be a **short-lived** experience. We should not be constantly self-examining ourselves since our focus is not to be on ourselves, but on Him. Even so, we should examine ourselves and judge ourselves from time to time as the Scriptures urge us to; however, it should be with the help of the Holy Spirit. We should let God search us and change us.

In Revelation chapters 2 and 3, Jesus showed the churches many places that needed changed. Yet, He ends each evaluation with *"He who has an ear, let him hear what the Spirit says to the churches."* It is the same today. Jesus is inviting us to change by hearing what the *Spirit* is saying that we need to change, not by our self-examination. We need to look to the Spirit and not to the knowledge of good and evil. We need to hear where we need to change by the voice of the Holy Spirit because He is our Helper, Comforter, Counselor, and "our Fixer."

Romans 2:4 says, *"the goodness of God leads you to repentance."* True repentance is change produced by God. Let the goodness of God lead you to change your life where needed.

His Faith

Jesus lived by His faith in God. He also expects us to live by faith. For we cannot please God apart from faith—it is impossible. *"And without faith it is impossible to please God . . ."* (Hebrews 11:6 NIV).

Jesus set the example for us by walking in faith, then He told us to, *"Have faith in God"* (see Mark 11:22). Furthermore, He said, *"If you can believe, all things are possible to him who believes"* (see Mark 9:23). Then Jesus shocked most when He said, *"Truly I say to you, He who puts his faith in me will do the very works which I do, and he will do greater things than these, because I am going to my Father"* (John 14:12 BBE).

His Humility

Jesus did not exalt Himself; He humbled Himself and set the example for us to follow. He was obedient to God from the heart in all things, and we are to let this same humble mind be in us.

> *Let this mind be in you which was also in Christ Jesus, who . . . humbled Himself and became obedient to the point of death, even the death of the cross. Therefore God also has highly exalted Him and given Him the name which is above every name.*
> *(Philippians 2:5–9)*

Humility carries great authority in heaven and earth. The most respected covering in heaven is that which Jesus clothed Himself with—humility. True authority is entrusted to the humble.

> *. . . Yes, all of you be submissive to one another, and be clothed with humility, for*
>
> *"God resists the proud,*
> *But gives grace to the humble."*
>
> *Therefore humble yourselves under the mighty hand of God, that He may exalt you in due time. (1 Peter 5:5–6)*

One of the greatest things that you can grow in is humility. Therefore, God will allow humbling opportunities to come to you—embrace them and grow in Christ.

The Picture

A picture is worth a thousand words, and Jesus is the picture of how to live as a human being on this earth. He is the complete picture with every "puzzle piece" in place. If you have any questions on how to live your life, seek Him. See how He lived His life. He is your example. Live your life to the fullest by following Jesus. He is the Path you are called to walk, but you do not walk alone, He sent His Holy Spirit as your helper, *"for it is God who works in you to will and to act according to his good purpose"* (Philippians 2:13 NIV).

A major key for growth is found in the two words of Jesus—*"Follow Me."* Enter into that **rest** of following in His footsteps. He set the path for us, we simply follow the Way—Jesus.

Now What?

Father, I thank You not just for saving me, but also for sending Jesus to live as a man setting the example of how I should live. I want to be like Jesus, but I can't do it in my own strength. Since You already know this, You gave me the Holy Spirit to help me. I ask for Your grace to enable me to lean on the Holy Spirit's power in order to live like Jesus. You know that too many times I act as if I don't want to live as Jesus did. However, I want You to help me live like Jesus even when I don't think I want to. I give You permission to work in me to will and to act like Jesus. I ask for these things in Your Son's name. Amen.

Then Jesus said to them, "Follow Me, and I will make you become fishers of men."

Mark 1:17

Chapter 7

The Adventure

Y ou took the first step to eternity when you were born again. Now what do you do? Is your life now complete since you are born again? Do you just sit back and wait to die and go to heaven? Is there something far greater to experience in this life before you die? Does God expect something more from you?

The Bible has the answer to these questions, and the purpose of this book is to show you what comes after salvation. Your salvation is only the beginning of the greatest adventure available to man. Will you go on to experience this adventure of a lifetime? The choice is yours to make. I invite you to make the choice to grow in Christ—to experience the greatest adventure possible. You're created for it; now go for it!

God—the Greatest Writer

God has written a script for your life; it is your destiny. Will you follow the script God has written for you? If you do, it will be the absolute greatest possible outcome for your life. Without question, your greatest adventure will be what God has desired for you to walk in. Follow Him and you will never be without adventure. You will not live an unfulfilling life, but will experience the joy of following Jesus Christ.

Let the Adventure Begin

Some think life begins at birth. Some think life begins at conception. Some think life begins before either of these. All of these views contain truth. Let's look at each one of these views.

First, the life begins at birth view contains truth because it is the beginning stage of the person's ability to live their life individually. The person is now separate from their mother and immediately begins to establish their own life even though they are very dependent upon others.

Second, the life begins at conception view has truth because it is the beginning, the start, the origin of pregnancy. God considers the embryo alive when there is blood. For the Scriptures declare that the life is in the blood. If there is blood, there is life.

Third, life begins before either of these first two views includes truth because of what the Scriptures show. God told Jeremiah:

> *Before I formed you in the womb I knew*
> *   you;*
> *Before you were born I sanctified you;*
> *I ordained you a prophet to the nations.*
> *   (Jeremiah 1:5)*

There are several instances in the Bible where God foretells the birth of individuals long before they were born. The most famous example is the birth of Jesus by a virgin. In addition to this, all human beings born and yet to be born are *in* Adam, the first man—*"For as in*

Adam all die" (1 Corinthians 15:22). Then the verse goes on to speak of those that are now *in* Christ, *"even so in Christ all shall be made alive."* All of humanity's adventure started when Adam was created. But there is a greater adventure for those who are in Christ. For God made it possible for those in Christ to get the most out of life by sending Jesus to show us the way. Just as we were *in* Adam by way of our humanity, now we are *in* Christ by way of our new birth. For sure, greater adventures are possible in Christ than are possible in Adam. In fact, there seems to be no limit on your adventures in Christ!

Jesus became a human being showing us how to get the most from life. He gave us the key to experiencing this full life when He declared:

> *Therefore do not worry, saying, "What shall we eat?" or "What shall we drink?" or "What shall we wear?" For after all these things the Gentiles seek. For your heavenly Father knows that you need all these things. But seek first the kingdom of God and His righteousness, and all these things shall be added to you. (Matthew 6:31–33)*

When we believe that *everything* we need and search for is found in God, we will seek Him willfully and diligently. Then He says that He will add all these things to us if we do not seek them, but seek Him. When we do this—seek *first* the kingdom of God and His righteousness—we will quickly grow.

So do you want to live this great adventure? You can. The Bible gives examples of all kinds of people living their life to the fullest regardless of their background. Moses murdered a man, but God called him to lead a multitude out of Egypt with many signs and wonders. By faith he lead Israel through the Red Sea on dry ground and when the Egyptians tried it, they drowned (see Hebrews 11:29).

A Samaritan woman who had five husbands and wasn't even married to the man she was living with, became the first evangelist (see John 4). Rahab the prostitute saved her whole family by her faith (see Joshua 2). It does not matter whether you have had a "good background" or a "bad background," God can do great things through anyone willing to follow Him. For our Father God gets great joy out of giving us the things of the kingdom. Jesus declared this plainly:

> *But seek the kingdom of God, and all these things shall be added to you.*
>
> *Do not fear, little flock, for it is your Father's good pleasure to give you the kingdom. (Luke 12:31–32)*

You do not have to fear missing anything when you seek first the kingdom of God since His kingdom is the fullness of life and adventure. Your life will be an amazing journey. However, not everyone will have the same degree of adventures. Your journey will be equal to your heart's capacity for adventure because not everyone enjoys the same type of exciting or risky activity. God knows what you like and He will gladly keep your life from boredom. When you are in God's plan for your life, you will be satisfied to the fullest, even on this side of heaven.

Walk with God

What would it be like to walk with a President? Or a king? Or the most famous person you may think of? Yet, that would be as nothing compared to walking with *God*. It is a fact; humans were created for the adventure of walking with **God!** Enoch walked with God for three hundred years and then God took him straight to heaven (see Genesis 5:22). What a glorious example for us—to walk with God for a lifetime.

When Jesus walked the earth, some left *everything* to follow Him, because there is no greater adventure than walking with God. We are all called to walk with God, to be a disciplined follower—a disciple. A disciple is one who will live the greatest adventure—walking with God.

God wants to help you to be you. He created you in His image. If you will mold yourself after Him and not after others, you can truly be all you can be and have great adventures in Him. He created these adventures just for you. Foremost, He created you to please Him. You please Him by believing in Him and following His will for your life. When you please Him, you will receive the most pleasure, and you will be more pleasing to others.

Desire

Where did the desire for more originate? Did it originate with God, man, or the devil? The answer to this question will influence your attitude toward the desire you have for more.

Let's begin at the beginning. In the beginning of the Bible, we see God creating the heavens and the earth. Why? Because He wanted more. The creation came about because God wanted more than what was.

When God saw everything more that He made, He was very satisfied. Included in that creation was God creating man in His own image—male and female (see Genesis 1:27). Since humans are created in God's image, they also have within them the desire for more. We see God confirming this desire when He says, *"Be fruitful and multiply; fill the earth and subdue it . . ."* (Genesis 1:28). Humans are to keep multiplying until they fill the earth and to keep taking dominion over it until they subdue it. They are never to stop multiplying until the earth is filled and they are never to stop taking dominion over the things of the earth until it is subdued. Thus, the desire for more comes from God.

Holy Desire

It seems everyone wants the most out of their life, and rightfully so. Getting the most out of your life is not only possible, it is the expectation and hope of the One who created you. If your Creator deposited within you that very desire at the moment of your creation, then your desire for more out of life is one of your most holy desires because it came from God.

Never be ashamed of your deep desire for more, it is God's gift to you so that He can fill you. Jesus called those that desire more, blessed, because they will be filled:

> *Blessed are those who hunger and thirst*
>   *for righteousness,*
> *For they shall be filled.*
>   *(Matthew 5:6)*

God did not just create in you the desire for more, He provided the Way to obtain more—growing in Christ.

Misused Desire

The devil knew that humanity had a God-given desire for more and that is how he tempted Adam and Eve. The devil used Eve's desire for more to tempt her to eat from the tree of the knowledge of good and evil. He said to her:

> *"God knows that your eyes will be opened as soon as you eat it, and you will be like God, knowing both good and evil."*
>
> *The woman was convinced. She saw that the tree was beautiful and its fruit looked delicious, and she wanted the wisdom it would give her. So she took some of the fruit and ate it. Then she gave some to her husband, who was with her, and he ate it, too. (Genesis 3:5–6 NLT)*

The Scripture above shows that Eve ate the fruit because she wanted the wisdom it would give her. It would give her something more than she had. Thus, the devil played on Adam and Eve's desire for more.

Our desire for more may cause us to give in to temptation. Temptation comes from desires within us. That does not mean that we should give up the desire for more. It means we have to be on guard not to give in to evil. The Scripture says:

> *The temptation to give in to evil comes from us and only us. We have no one to blame but the leering, seducing flare-up of our own lust. (James 1:14 TMSG)*

Ultimate Desire

The devil played on the ultimate desire of humanity with Adam and Eve. Knowing that humanity's greatest desire is to be like God, the devil used that to tempt Eve saying:

> *God knows that the moment you eat from that tree, you'll see what's really going on. You'll be just like God, knowing everything, ranging all the way from good to evil. (Genesis 3:5 TMSG)*

Eve did not just want the wisdom; she wanted the wisdom of God—to be like God. But only God can make you like Him and He has provided everything you need for that purpose. 2 Peter 1:4 states:

> *By which have been given to us exceedingly great and precious promises, that through these you may be partakers of the divine*

nature, having escaped the corruption that is
in the world through lust.

Humans were created with an ultimate desire inside them—to be like God. This is the highest calling and the ultimate adventure.

God made Adam and Eve in His image, His likeness, and there was only one way not to be like Him—to do what He said not to do. When they disobeyed, it caused a separation between God and them that only He could fix.

Deception

The devil can only deceive humankind if he can get them to question and doubt what God says. God said that eating from the tree of the knowledge of good and evil would cause death (see Genesis 2:17). But the devil contradicted God's word, *"Then the serpent said to the woman, 'You will not surely die.'"* (Genesis 3:4). The woman believed him, and doubted God's word. Eve was deceived when she believed she could be like God by doing the very thing that separated her from God. Deception believes the lie instead of the truth. The devil is called "the father of lies," and Jesus is called "the Truth." You can either believe the liar or you can believe the Truth—Jesus.

It is not a sin to be tempted. The sin is in yielding to the temptation. Jesus never sinned, but He was tempted. He was tempted when the Holy Spirit led Him into the wilderness to be tested by the devil. After the Father had just proclaimed that He was His beloved Son, Jesus was tempted by the devil saying, *"If You are the Son of God.*" But Jesus chose to believe God instead of the devil (see Matthew 3:17–4:4). He was not deceived. If we will follow Jesus, we can be kept from deception, but not from temptation.

Adventure of Faith

One of the main characteristics of Jesus' life was His faith in God the Father. We are to follow His example— faith toward God. What can our faith accomplish? The same thing Jesus' faith achieved. This is found in 1 John 3:8, "*. . . For this purpose the Son of God was manifested, that He might destroy the works of the devil.*"

The biggest work of the devil was when he destroyed the relationship between God and humanity. However, Jesus restored our relationship to God through the cross. Forgiveness of all our sins is at the cross.

> *You were dead because of your sins and because your sinful nature was not yet cut away. Then God made you alive with Christ, for he forgave all our sins. He canceled the record of the charges against us and took it away by nailing it to the cross. In this way, he disarmed the spiritual rulers and authorities. He shamed them publicly by his victory over them on the cross. (Colossians 2:13–15 NLT)*

By our faith in what Jesus did on the cross, our relationship to God is restored—we are born again through our faith (see Ephesians 2:8). The Bible stresses the importance of our faith in many verses, such as Romans 4:16, *"Therefore it is of faith that it might be according to grace, so that the promise might be sure to all . . ."*

Our faith toward God is of upmost importance. It is through our faith that God's saving grace is released. Then when we are reconciled to God, we are given the great adventure of the ministry of reconciliation—getting others to be right with God.

> *God has given us the task of telling everyone what he is doing. We're Christ's representatives. God uses us to persuade men and women to drop their differences and enter into God's work of making things right between them. We're speaking for Christ himself now: Become friends with God; he's already a friend with you. (2 Corinthians 5:19–20 TMSG)*

Being reconciled to God is the most important part of our adventure, but it is only the beginning of our faith. Our faith can accomplish many more things. There is even a whole chapter in the Bible devoted to what men and women accomplished by faith (see Hebrews 11). One of my favorite accomplishments is found in verse 35, *"Women received their dead raised to life again."* Yes, faith toward God destroys the work of the devil.

You will also need faith toward God because your life's great adventure will be like a roller coaster ride—

there will be highs and lows. You will need to learn how to abound and how to be abased—how to be content.

> . . . for I have learned in whatever state I am,
> to be content: I know how to be abased, and
> I know how to abound. Everywhere and in
> all things I have learned both to be full and
> to be hungry, both to abound and to suffer
> need. I can do all things through Christ who
> strengthens me. (Philippians 4:11–13)

Live the life God has for you; enjoy the ride!

Review

The last four chapters: *The Challenge, The Answer, The Example,* and *The Adventure,* dealt with the first of the basic principles of following Christ—repentance from dead works and faith toward God. This is the most important of the basic principles because it is the beginning of your life in Christ. By turning from trusting in your own works to trusting in God's work, you have the greatest growth potential possible. In fact, growing in Christ is the greatest adventure!

The next several chapters will explain the rest of the basic principles of our growth in Christ.

Now What?

Father, I believe Your plan for my life is greater than my plan. So help me to choose Your plan, to follow You. Forgive me for the times I have resisted Your direction for my life. For I do not always understand that Your plans are the absolute best for me. I want to trust You more. I want to move in faith and do what You call me to do.

Holy Spirit, help me to hunger for the more that the Father has for me. I want more—more growth in Christ. But I also need You to help me to see the need that others have for more of You. Help me to help others receive more of Christ. In His name I pray. Amen.

God, who got you started in this spiritual adventure, shares with us the life of his Son and our Master Jesus. He will never give up on you. Never forget that.

1 Corinthians 1:9 TMSG

Chapter 8

Baptisms

*B*aptisms should not be one of the most controversial subjects. Nevertheless, it is because there is a lack of comprehending the value of baptisms. When we understand baptisms' value to our growth in Christ, there should not be so much controversy.

The first thing to notice about baptisms is that the word is in the plural. There is more than one baptism. It is a sad fact that many born-again believers do not even know there are multiple baptisms even though it is one of the basic principles of Christ. Even if you know there are several baptisms, this chapter can help your growth in Christ through establishing the basic principles of these baptisms.

Baptisms are the next most important basic principle of Christ after repentance from dead works and faith toward God—the starting point of your Christian life. Why are they the next most important? Because they are the empowering for your growth in Christ. Without understanding the basic principle of these baptisms, your growth may be extremely limited. However, if you understand and experience these baptisms, growing in Christ will be much faster and easier.

It is not in the scope of this chapter to explain these baptisms as they deserve, so we will only briefly consider five of them.

Water

When some hear the word *baptism*, they only think of water baptism. Before we go further, what does the word *baptism* mean? Baptism means: to dip, to immerse, to submerge. Thus, water baptism is to go under water. Why would we need to do that? Foremost because Jesus commanded it:

> *Therefore, go and make disciples of all the nations, baptizing them in the name of the Father and the Son and the Holy Spirit. Teach these new disciples to obey all the commands I have given you. . . . (Matthew 28:19–20 NLT)*

Jesus' disciples set the example of obedience to His command to baptize with water all throughout the book of Acts. Of course, they understood the importance of water baptism. For example, when Peter gave his message on the Day of Pentecost, people were convicted and wanted to know what they should do.

> *Now when they heard this, they were cut to the heart, and said to Peter and the rest of the apostles, "Men and brethren, what shall we do?"*
>
> *Then Peter said to them, "Repent, and let every one of you be baptized in the name of*

Jesus Christ for the remission of sins . . ."
(Acts 2:37–38)

Both men and women were water baptized (see Acts 8:12). Even so, water baptism is only intended for believers in Jesus Christ. Philip confirmed this in Acts 8.

> *Now as they went down the road, they came to some water. And the eunuch said, "See, here is water. What hinders me from being baptized?"*
>
> *Then Philip said, "If you believe with all your heart, you may."*
>
> *And he answered and said, "I believe that Jesus Christ is the Son of God."*
>
> *So he commanded the chariot to stand still. And both Philip and the eunuch went down into the water, and he baptized him. (Acts 8:36–38)*

What is the significance of water baptism? It is to be one of the *first* acts of obedience when someone believes on Jesus Christ, as seen all through the New Testament. They would believe and then be water baptized. If you have not been water baptized, then you have not obeyed Jesus in this matter. What is the significance of that? Besides the fact that when you do not get water baptized, even though Jesus commanded it, you are disobeying Him; the Scriptures connect water baptism to cleansing from sin (see Acts 2:38; 22:16; Romans 6).

> *. . . When we went under the water, we left the old country of sin behind; when we came up out of the water, we entered into the new country of grace—a new life in a new land!*
>
> *That's what baptism into the life of Jesus means. When we are lowered into the water, it is like the burial of Jesus; when we are raised up out of the water, it is like the resurrection of Jesus. . . .*
>
> *Could it be any clearer? Our old way of life was nailed to the Cross with Christ, a decisive end to that sin-miserable life—no longer at sin's every beck and call! What we believe is this: If we get included in Christ's sin-conquering death, we also get included in his life-saving resurrection. (Romans 6:3– 8 TMSG)*

There is a spiritual connection between water baptism and the burial of sin. Consequently, water baptism can help you in your growth in Christ since sin hinders growth. Therefore you should be water baptized shortly after being born again.

Water baptism is also a public expression of our commitment to Christ—that we are willing to lay down our lives for Him and to live a new life in Him.

This is not a comprehensive teaching on water baptism. Yet, those in the New Testament did not have it carefully explained; still, they obeyed, knowing that Jesus commanded it.

Holy Spirit

The human race is forever connected to God because they were made in His image. In addition, God is forever connected to the human race because Jesus became a man. When He became the Son of Man and lived among us, He no longer wanted us to be without His *personal* presence. Therefore God the Father gave Jesus the promise that we would not be left alone. The Father promised that He would send the Holy Spirit to us after He (Jesus) returned to heaven. Moreover, He would not just send the Holy Spirit, but He would *baptize* us in the Holy Spirit.

> *And being assembled together with them, [Jesus] commanded them not to depart from Jerusalem, but to wait for the Promise of the Father, "which," He said, "you have heard from Me; for John truly baptized with water, but you shall be baptized with the Holy Spirit not many days from now." (Acts 1:4–5)*

The baptism of the Holy Spirit is the greatest power you have for growth. For the Holy Spirit will teach you all things and remind you of everything that Jesus said (see John 14:26). Jesus said that He had to leave for the Holy Spirit to come. He also said it is *best* for us that He left and that the Holy Spirit came (see John 16:7).

The Holy Spirit is power and when we are baptized in Him, we are *mightily* empowered. This power is especially for telling people about Jesus—for living a life that is a witness to Jesus—a holy (set apart) life.

> *But you will receive power when the Holy*
> *Spirit comes on you; and you will be my*
> *witnesses in Jerusalem, and in all Judea and*
> *Samaria, and to the ends of the earth. (Acts*
> *1:8 NIV)*

Our need for the baptism in the Holy Spirit should be emphasized to us when we are born again. For it is the Holy Spirit that enables us to live holy and to inspire others to holiness—to grow in Christ.

If you are born again, then the promise of the baptism of the Holy Spirit is for you. Don't let anyone talk you out of the very power to live your life for Christ.

> *Then Peter said to them, "Repent, and let*
> *every one of you be baptized in the name of*
> *Jesus Christ for the remission of sins; and*
> *you shall receive the gift of the Holy Spirit.*
> *For the promise is to you and to your*
> *children, and to all who are afar off, as*
> *many as the Lord our God will call." (Acts*
> *2:38–39)*

If you are born again, God has called you and the promise of the baptism of the Holy Spirit is for you. When you receive the baptism of the Spirit, you can speak in a language you have never learned (see Acts 2:4). Why would you want to do that? So that you can speak directly to God from your spirit and not just your mind. As a result, you're praying a perfect prayer in the will of God by the Holy Spirit.

And in the same way the Spirit is a help to our feeble hearts: for we are not able to make prayer to God in the right way; but the Spirit puts our desires into words which are not in our power to say;

And he who is the searcher of hearts has knowledge of the mind of the Spirit, because he is making prayers for the saints in agreement with the mind of God. (Romans 8:26-27 BBE)

Another reason for praying in a language that you do not know (tongues) is for the building up of your faith. Jude says, *"But you, dear friends, carefully build yourselves up in this most holy faith by praying in the Holy Spirit"* (Jude 20 TMSG).

Still another reason for speaking in tongues is that it is confirmation to others that you have been baptized in the Holy Spirit. It showed the early Christians that the baptism of the Spirit is not just for the Jews but for non-Jews (Gentiles) as well.

While Peter was still speaking these words, the Holy Spirit fell upon all those who heard the word. And those of the circumcision who believed were astonished, as many as came with Peter, because the gift of the Holy Spirit had been poured out on the Gentiles also. For they heard them speak with tongues and magnify God. (Acts 10:44–46)

Yet another reason for speaking in tongues is that it exalts God. When God gives a person the power to speak a language they do not know, they magnify Him. Having received the baptism of the Spirit, I can testify that it brings a deeper exaltation of God.

Even though you are born again, this may be the first time you have heard of the baptism of the Holy Spirit. If this is the case, then now is the time for you to be asked one of the most important questions in the Bible: *"Did you receive the Holy Spirit when you believed?"* (see Acts 19:2–6).

Because some do not understand how wonderful the gift of the Holy Spirit with tongues is, I want to end this section with the Scriptural exhortation: *"don't forbid speaking in tongues"* (see 1 Corinthians 14:39).

The Bible has much more to say about the baptism of the Holy Spirit and about speaking in tongues than what I can explain in this chapter. Thus, I would recommend a deeper study on this subject.

Fire

When you hear the word *fire*, it may make you think of either a destructive force or a soothing, comforting warmth. How you are thinking of fire right now will determine your reaction to this question: "Do you want a baptism of fire?"

I hope that your answer is, "Yes!" If not, then it may be after we explain what it is. First, let's look at the promise of the baptism of fire. John the Baptist told us that Jesus would baptize us in fire saying, *"He will baptize you with the Holy Spirit and fire"* (Matthew 3:11).

The thing I notice first in this verse is that Jesus is the One baptizing us in fire. Since it comes from Jesus, it has to be good for us. Why? The answer is found in the last book of the Old Testament.

> *. . . Then suddenly the Lord you are seeking will come to his temple . . .*
>
> *But who can endure the day of his coming? Who can stand when he appears? For he will be like a refiner's fire or a launderer's soap. He will sit as a refiner and purifier of silver; he will purify the Levites and refine them like gold and silver. Then the Lord will have men who will bring offerings in righteousness.* *(Malachi 3:1–3 NIV)*

Jesus comes with the baptism of fire to remove the impurities in our lives. Even so, He does not see us as impure, but as gold and silver that simply needs the impurities removed. We are precious to Him, so He does not want anything hindering our beauty. His baptism of fire beautifies us; it cleanses us like a launderer's soap.

The baptism of fire is actually a baptism in His love. Love is the most consuming force. It will consume everything that is unnecessary in a person's life. We probably have seen someone or experienced being so in love ourselves that everything else becomes unimportant. Only what, or whom, we are in love with matters. This is what the baptism of fire is for—to make us single minded toward God. It will consume all the impurities in our life, leaving only the pure. After that, as the Scripture above states, *"Then the Lord will have men who will bring offerings in righteousness."*

The baptism of fire will bring conviction of sin. The sin it will convict us of is our lack of love. For when we see pure love (God) we will be convicted of falling short of His glory—His love. When you see God, you will know you need cleansed. What is the biggest cleansing we need? The same cleansing as the prophet Isaiah needed after seeing God:

> . . . *"Woe is me, for I am undone!*
> *Because I am a man of unclean lips,*
> *And I dwell in the midst of a people of*
>   *unclean lips;*
> *For my eyes have seen the King,*
> *The Lord of hosts."*
>
> *Then one of the seraphim flew to me, having in his hand a live coal which he had taken with the tongs from the altar. And he touched my mouth with it, and said:*
>
> *"Behold, this has touched your lips;*
> *Your iniquity is taken away,*
> *And your sin purged."*
>   *(Isaiah 6:5–7)*

The fiery coal from the altar, the fire of God, purified Isaiah's tongue, which enabled him to go and proclaim the word of the Lord. We all need our tongues purified so we can be a blessing to others. This is the same message James gave to the church:

For we all stumble in many things. If anyone does not stumble in word, he is a perfect man, able also to bridle the whole body. . . . And the tongue is a fire, a world of iniquity. The tongue is so set among our members that it defiles the whole body, and sets on fire the course of nature; and it is set on fire by hell. . . . But no man can tame the tongue. It is an unruly evil, full of deadly poison. With it we bless our God and Father, and with it we curse men, who have been made in the similitude of God. Out of the same mouth proceed blessing and cursing. My brethren, these things ought not to be so. Does a spring send forth fresh water and bitter from the same opening? (James 3:2–11)

No man can tame the tongue; it takes the baptism of fire like Isaiah experienced. It takes God purging our mouth with His fire. I believe this is why the Holy Spirit appeared as tongues of fire over those that received the baptism of the Holy Spirit on the Day of Pentecost (see Acts 2:3). He was purifying their tongues for sharing the wonderful works of God. He did not want fresh water and bitter water coming from their mouths. For when you receive the Holy Spirit, rivers of living water flow out of your heart.

He who believes in Me, as the Scripture has said, out of his heart will flow rivers of living water. But this He spoke concerning the

Spirit, whom those believing in Him would
receive . . . (John 7:38–39)

This baptism creates a fire within you for being a witness to Jesus. It compels you to share the great things of God. If you have this fire within you and try to quench it, you will understand what Jeremiah experienced:

> *Then I said, "I will not make mention of*
>   *Him,*
> *Nor speak anymore in His name."*
> *But His word was in my heart like a*
>   *burning fire*
> *Shut up in my bones;*
> *I was weary of holding it back,*
> *And I could not.*
>   *(Jeremiah 20:9)*

The baptism of fire frees us to grow abundantly in Christ since it removes the impurities that can hinder our growth. We need the baptism of fire for the sake of everyone who will ever hear us speak. God help us with Your fire!

Suffering

The baptism of suffering is one of the most misunderstood of the baptisms. Why? Because too many think that suffering means that you have done something wrong and are therefore suffering the consequences for it. Of course, this could be true, but it is not as true as we think. The suffering may be something we are baptized into. To know this sets us free from trying to "figure out what we did wrong."

> But Jesus said to them, ". . . Are you able to drink from the bitter cup of suffering I am about to drink? Are you able to be baptized with the baptism of suffering I must be baptized with?"
>
> "Oh yes," they replied, "we are able!"
>
> Then Jesus told them, "You will indeed drink from my bitter cup and be baptized with my baptism of suffering." (Mark 10:38–39 NLT)

Some include this baptism of suffering as a part of the baptism of fire. I would not argue with this, but by separating them, the revelation of each one is clearer. So what exactly does this baptism of suffering mean? Jesus informs us that we will suffer as He did. He was persecuted and we will be too. Jesus said:

> If the world hates you, you know that it hated Me before it hated you. If you were of the world, the world would love its own. Yet because you are not of the world, but I chose you out of the world, therefore the world hates you. Remember the word that I said to you, "A servant is not greater than his master. If they persecuted Me, they will also persecute you. . . ."
>
> These things I have spoken to you, that you should not be made to stumble. They will put you out of the synagogues; yes, the time is

> coming that whoever kills you will think
> that he offers God service. (John 15:18–20;
> 16:1–2)

Jesus informs us that we will suffer so that when it happens we will not stumble over it. In fact, suffering on the behalf of Christ is His gift to us:

> There's far more to this life than trusting in
> Christ. There's also suffering for him. And
> the suffering is as much a gift as the trusting.
> (Philippians 1:29 TMSG)

Any gift Jesus gives us is more valuable than we can comprehend. This is especially true of the gift of suffering. For there is a special fellowship with Christ when we suffer what He suffered. Our friendship goes deeper because of our fellowship in His sufferings.

Abraham was called the friend of God (see James 2:23) and he experienced the fellowship of sufferings. God revealed His deepest secret to Abraham—that He would sacrifice His Son for humankind (see John 8:56). Then He allowed Abraham to have the privilege of experiencing this same suffering. That is, Abraham experienced the fellowship of the suffering of sacrificing a son. Although God stopped Abraham just before he killed his son Isaac, Abraham still experienced the suffering of sacrificing the son he loved so much. Through Abraham's act of obedience, there was a special fellowship between him and God—they both knew what it felt like to sacrifice their son for another.

God gave to Abraham this special intimacy (in-to-me-see) by granting him the fellowship of the suffering of sacrificing their unique sons (God sacrificed Jesus; Abraham sacrificed Isaac). This intimacy solidified their friendship—took it to a completely new level.

This is true of all that have suffered similar things. For we are able to understand and comfort someone who has suffered as we have, and we can have a special fellowship and friendship with him or her.

> *God is our merciful Father and the source of all comfort. He comforts us in all our troubles so that we can comfort others. When they are troubled, we will be able to give them the same comfort God has given us. (2 Corinthians 1:3–4 NLT)*

When we suffer the same things Christ suffered, we have a special fellowship with Him. We have a special intimacy. We understand how each other feels by going through the same things. Jesus understands our weaknesses because he faced all of the same things we do (see Hebrews 4:15). Therefore we can have a close friendship with Jesus because we have experienced similar things.

There are different kinds of suffering. We will only mention a couple here. First, we may suffer on the behalf of others—for His church. *"I now rejoice in my sufferings for you, and fill up in my flesh what is lacking in the afflictions of Christ, for the sake of His body, which is the church"* (Colossians 1:24).

Second, as Jesus stated, others may cause us to suffer—especially our families:

I came to send fire on the earth, and how I wish it were already kindled! But I have a baptism to be baptized with, and how distressed I am till it is accomplished! Do you suppose that I came to give peace on earth? I tell you, not at all, but rather division. For from now on five in one house will be divided: three against two, and two against three. Father will be divided against son and son against father, mother against daughter and daughter against mother, mother-in-law against her daughter-in-law and daughter-in-law against her mother-in-law. (Luke 12:49–53)

It is contrary to Scripture and to the experience of countless saints to believe that Christians are not to suffer. In fact, sufferings are valuable for our growth. Even Jesus learned obedience by the things He suffered. *"Though He was a Son, yet He learned obedience by the things which He suffered"* (Hebrews 5:8).

To know that suffering is a part of your life in Christ may keep you from choosing the path of least resistance—the easy way. The easy way is not usually God's way. The easy way only looks easy, but often quickly turns into a hard way. But what appears as the hard way is often God's way, which may even turn out to be the easy way. Whether God's way is easy or hard, it is always the best way.

As we all know, it is much easier to obey when it costs little. However, obedience that costs everything is the obedience that Jesus learned. Even so, in His suffering He experienced true joy. Yes, He suffered and experienced joy at the same time (see Hebrews 12:2). I experienced this once when I was suffering. I felt such joy and gratitude to God for allowing me to suffer with Christ. It made no sense to my mind that my spirit was full of joy even when my body was suffering.

If we suffer with Him, we will also reign with Him (see 2 Timothy 2:12). Our baptism of suffering is to prepare us for reigning with Him—even to be able to judge angels.

Too many have become offended with God when they experience suffering, which stifles their growth. Don't be one of them. Embrace the baptism of suffering and grow into all Jesus wants you to be.

His Body

The first thing that God said was not good was when Adam was alone. *"Then the Lord God said, 'It is not good for the man to be alone. I will make a helper who is just right for him'"* (Genesis 2:18 NLT). The same is true for every one of us—it is not good for us to be alone.

When we are born again, God does something very special for us. He baptizes us into the body of Christ— the church. Even though many of us have not understood the importance of this baptism, God does; therefore He baptizes us into the church—the body of Christ. Why? Because we are not meant to be alone, but to be joined with other believers in a living relationship. We are immersed, baptized into the body of believers.

> *. . . But we have all been baptized into one body by one Spirit, and we all share the same Spirit. (1 Corinthians 12:13 NLT)*

This baptism, like all the others we have mentioned, is vital for our growth. Without the essential connection to the body, we will not develop properly since it takes the interaction within the body of Christ for our full development. There will be challenges, disagreements, and hard times, as in all relationships, but these are all part of what it takes for our proper growth.

It is no accident that the "love chapter" (1 Corinthians 13) follows the "body of Christ chapter" (1 Corinthians 12), because it takes our love of God and others to grow as we should. I want to say it as plainly as I can—you must be baptized into a local fellowship of believers to grow as God intended.

> *The way God designed our bodies is a model for understanding our lives together as a church: every part dependent on every other part, the parts we mention and the parts we don't, the parts we see and the parts we don't. If one part hurts, every other part is involved in the hurt, and in the healing. If one part flourishes, every other part enters into the exuberance.*
>
> *You are Christ's body—that's who you are! You must never forget this. Only as you accept your part of that body does your "part" mean anything. (1 Corinthians 12:25– 27 TMSG)*

If you think you can grow as you should without a living relationship with the body of Christ, know that the Scriptures declare otherwise. Too many believers are not in a vital relationship to a church, which is sad for them and for the church that God intended for them to be a part of. We need each other. We all need to "grow up" and become the body of Christ He intended. Hear the heartbeat of God as He confronts us with these words:

> *If you've gotten anything at all out of following Christ, if his love has made any difference in your life, if being in a community of the Spirit means anything to you, if you have a heart, if you care—then do me a favor: Agree with each other, love each other, be deep-spirited friends. Don't push your way to the front; don't sweet-talk your way to the top. Put yourself aside, and help others get ahead. Don't be obsessed with getting your own advantage. Forget yourselves long enough to lend a helping hand. (Philippians 2:1–4 TMSG)*

Don't wait for everyone to love you perfectly, for it will never happen (not on this side of heaven). You be the one who loves others as you should. You set the example for others, not letting their actions keep you from loving. As the verse above says, *"Put yourself aside, and help others get ahead."* You be the leader in love and friendship. As Proverbs 18:24 states, *"A man who has friends must himself be friendly."*

The New Testament letters to the churches show that there has yet to be a "perfect church." Even so, we must be baptized into the body of Christ for the sake of our growth and the growth of others. Far too many believers have stopped growing in Jesus because they become offended with the body of Christ—the church. Do not be as the person described in Proverbs 18:19:

> An offended brother is more unyielding than a fortified city, and disputes are like the barred gates of a citadel. (NIV)

If you have been offended by the church, and we all have, take it to Jesus who understands what it is like to be hurt and betrayed even by a close friend. Remember, Judas Iscariot stole money from Jesus (see John 12:6) and betrayed Him in Gethsemane *with a kiss.*

But God invites you to be what He has called you to be even if others don't respond properly:

> Therefore, as God's chosen people, holy and dearly loved, clothe yourselves with compassion, kindness, humility, gentleness and patience. Bear with each other and forgive whatever grievances you may have against one another. Forgive as the Lord forgave you. And over all these virtues put on love, which binds them all together in perfect unity. (Colossians 3:12–14 NIV)

Now What?

Father, I want to pray for Your help, but first I must acknowledge that You have already given me more help than I am using. Therefore I pray that You would help me to use the help You have baptized me with—in water, the Holy Spirit, fire, suffering, and Jesus' body.

I want to pray as Paul did in Philippians 3:10—*"That I may know Him and the power of His resurrection, and the fellowship of His sufferings."* However, I can only pray this half-heartedly because I do not like to suffer. But I do want the special fellowship that comes in the suffering.

Father, You know the special times we have had during suffering, therefore, Papa, Father, not what I will, but what You will. For the best fellowship I have had with Jesus has come during suffering. So help me Holy Spirit to remember Jesus' sufferings on my behalf and the fellowship we have during suffering.

Help me not to hold onto any offense, but to forgive quickly. And help me to love others the way I want to be loved. In Jesus' name I pray. Amen.

John answered, saying to all, "I indeed baptize you with water; but One mightier than I is coming, whose sandal strap I am not worthy to loose. He will baptize you with the Holy Spirit and fire."

Luke 3:16

Chapter 9

Hands

*W*here would we be without hands? Hands have created countless objects all through the ages. Yet, hands are not necessary for your life. Several people have learned to live with one or no hands. Nevertheless, it makes life more difficult since God created hands to perform much of our daily needs and work. In fact, hands are equated with work. The creation is called the work of God's hands (Psalm 102:25) that includes the creation of man (Psalm 119:73). Even so, God's hands were not the source of the work. The work originated in His heart.

Our heart also directs the works of our hands. A large amount of what our heart desires, our hands carry out. Consequently, what our hands do can often show what is in our heart, and the heart determines what kind of hands we have—holy or unholy. So when God says to *"lift up holy hands,"* He is referring more to our heart than our hands.

Just as God's hands are an extension of His heart of love for all of creation, so our hands are to be an extension of our love. Thus, we can only fully accomplish God's purpose for creating our hands by loving the Lord and loving others. When we do not have love in our heart, first for God and then for others, our hands may easily be used for evil purposes.

Adam and Eve's hands did not cause them to sin when they took the forbidden fruit; it was their decision to disobey God. The sin came from the decision in their heart. Then their first-born son murdered his brother Abel with his *hand,* but Cain's hand was simply the extension of what was in his heart. For Cain was jealous because his works were evil while Abel's works were good. Therefore he hated Abel and killed him. Cain's hands worked evil because his heart was evil (see 1 John 3:12–14).

Love is the solution for keeping our hands holy. Without love for God and others, our hands may be used wickedly. In view of that, *love* should be the motivating factor in the use of our hands.

Laying on of Hands

The next basic principle of Christ listed in Hebrews 6:2 is the *laying on of hands.* This basic principle of Christ is also very important for our growth, because we all need what the laying on of hands can do for us.

The saints in the Old Testament knew the importance of the laying on of hands. They understood that God enabled their hands to impart blessings and even destiny to others. If you want to see a great example of this, you may read Genesis 48:8–20.

God is love and He desires to impart that love to others. He has chosen to use humans that have His heart of love to impart His blessings through the laying on of hands. You can impart His blessings to others by your hands. In addition, some of God's blessings will not come to *you* except through others laying their hands on you. Why? Because God has given man authority over the earth. Psalm 115:16 says, *"The heaven of heavens is for God, but he put us in charge of the earth"* (TMSG).

Recently in a prayer meeting while we were discussing and praying concerning this issue of humanity's responsibility in the Lord's work, the Lord gave my wife a vision of a backhoe. A backhoe is a powerful machine, but until someone begins to operate it, it just sits there. But when the operator uses his *hands* on the controls, the power is released. So it is in the kingdom of God at this time—our hands do the work but the real power is in the Holy Spirit. Even so, we are in the "driver's seat" and unless our hands operate the controls, the power is never released. That is why James 4:2 says, *"You do not have, because you do not ask God"* (NIV). God has given us the responsibility to ask for what we need.

A backhoe operator has to learn the "controls" to do a professional job, so we too must learn to follow the leading of the Holy Spirit to release His power in the best way possible. The next verse in James goes on to say, *"When you ask, you do not receive, because you ask with wrong motives, that you may spend what you get on your pleasures"* (James 4:3 NIV). It takes the schooling of the Holy Spirit to remove wrong attitudes and motives from our hearts just as it takes training to use a backhoe. The Lord needs to train us in the laying on of hands to be the most effective in it.

Furthermore, a backhoe operator does not just dig wherever he chooses, but where the "one in charge" directs, so we should only lay hands on others as the Holy Spirit directs. *"Do not be hasty in the laying on of hands, and do not share in the sins of others. Keep yourself pure"* (1 Timothy 5:22 NIV). Another translation of this verse says, *"Do not put hands on any man without thought, and have no part in other men's sins: keep yourself clean"* (BBE).

God wants others to lay hands on us and for us to lay hands on others—but carefully, not haphazardly. Why? Because the laying on of hands is for imparting things— good and bad. Still, do not become overly cautious, but have more faith in God to keep you safe than faith in the devil to hurt you.

The Power

The power of God is activated many times through the laying on of hands. We will look now at how Jesus laid hands on people, because no one used their hands more appropriately than Jesus did.

> *One day some parents brought their children to Jesus so he could lay his hands on them and pray for them. But the disciples scolded the parents for bothering him.*
>
> *But Jesus said, "Let the children come to me. Don't stop them! For the Kingdom of Heaven belongs to those who are like these children." And he placed his hands on their heads and*

blessed them before he left. (Matthew 19:13–
15 NLT)

We see that Jesus used the laying on of hands to especially pray and bless children. Nonetheless, all Christians are also His children that He wants to bless through the laying on of hands. However, He does not have His hands on earth now; we are now His hands on earth, therefore we are to pray and bless others through the laying on of our hands.

Can you imagine what a blessing these children received when Jesus laid His hands on them? He can do the same thing through our hands since He lives inside of us in the person of the Holy Spirit. Also, we can receive His blessings from others as they lay their hands on us.

We are "Jesus' physical hands" on the earth now and He wants to use our hands for the flow of His blessing to others. Yes, we are the only hands He has on earth now and He wants us to use them for pouring out His love.

When Jesus walked the earth, He healed many sicknesses through the laying on of His hands. Indeed, many marveled at the mighty works performed by His hands (see Mark 6:2). For instance, He raised a dead girl by His hands and with the words He spoke, which caused great amazement:

> . . . *"My little daughter lies at the point of death. Come and lay Your hands on her, that she may be healed, and she will live."*

> *. . . While He was still speaking, some came from the ruler of the synagogue's house who said, "Your daughter is dead. Why trouble the Teacher any further?"*
>
> *As soon as Jesus heard the word that was spoken, He said to the ruler of the synagogue, "Do not be afraid; only believe."*
>
> *. . . Then He took the child by the hand, and said to her, "Talitha, cumi," which is translated, "Little girl, I say to you, arise." Immediately the girl arose and walked, for she was twelve years of age. And they were overcome with great amazement. (Mark 5:23–42)*

It may take the laying on of hands more than once to see a complete result. We see this when Jesus healed a blind man's eyes. For He laid His hands on his eyes more than once to see the entire healing.

> *. . . Some people brought a sightless man and begged Jesus to give him a healing touch. Taking him by the hand, he led him out of the village. He put spit in the man's eyes, laid hands on him, and asked, "Do you see anything?"*
>
> *He looked up. "I see men. They look like walking trees." So Jesus laid hands on his eyes again. The man looked hard and realized that he had recovered perfect sight, saw everything in bright, twenty-twenty focus. (Mark 8:22–25 TMSG)*

Jesus also healed the deaf and mute through the laying on of hands (see Mark 7:32–35). Finally, Jesus was not even afraid to lay hands on unclean lepers and heal them.

> *Now a leper came to Him, imploring Him, kneeling down to Him and saying to Him, "If You are willing, You can make me clean."*
>
> *Then Jesus, moved with compassion, stretched out His hand and touched him, and said to him, "I am willing; be cleansed." As soon as He had spoken, immediately the leprosy left him, and he was cleansed. (Mark 1:40–43)*

Jesus' hands were for blessing—to do what was best for others and the kingdom of God. Our hands are for the same purpose—to be a blessing for others as well as His kingdom.

The disciples of Jesus followed Jesus' example and laid hands on many people. Even so, they recognized that it was God's hand working through them.

> *Now, Lord, look on their threats, and grant to Your servants that with all boldness they may speak Your word, by stretching out Your hand to heal, and that signs and wonders may be done through the name of Your holy Servant Jesus. (Acts 4:29–30)*

Pierced Hands

Jesus' hands were pierced. His hands are still nail-scarred. Why? Hands are synonymous with work and the greatest work Jesus did was on the cross. The nail-prints in His hands show that He is the One who sacrificed for us. The greatest thing His hands ever did was for our salvation. No greater love was ever expressed than when Jesus died on the cross for us. **God is love!** His nail-scarred hands prove it. Believe it; don't be a "doubting Thomas."

> But Thomas . . . said, "Unless I see the nail holes in his hands, put my finger in the nail holes, and stick my hand in his side, I won't believe it."

> Eight days later . . . Jesus came . . . he focused his attention on Thomas. "Take your finger and examine my hands. Take your hand and stick it in my side. Don't be unbelieving. Believe."

> Thomas said, "My Master! My God!"

> Jesus said, "So, you believe because you've seen with your own eyes. Even better blessings are in store for those who believe without seeing." (John 20:25–29 TMSG)

Other Blessings

The laying on of hands may also impart a commissioning or a gifting of the Holy Spirit. Paul imparted a ministry gift to Timothy through the laying on of hands. *"And the special gift of ministry you received when I laid hands on you and prayed—keep that ablaze!"* (2 Timothy 1:6 TMSG).

Any Christian no matter their age or gender can impart God's blessings through their hands, or have blessings imparted to them through another's hands. The laying on of hands is important for our growth in Christ, whether we are the one receiving or the one giving the laying on of hands.

Summary

The laying on of hands is about blessings and destiny. It is more than getting healed, getting a miracle, or an impartation. It is about touching, feeling, or experiencing the love of God. When you are prayed for with the laying on of hands and you receive a blessing, you are experiencing the love and care of God for you. When you pray for someone else with the laying on of hands, they are experiencing the love of God as He blesses them through you.

The laying on of hands is for touching your destiny. For your destiny is to experience the personal love and care of God, and the love and care of others. Of course, this will be your experience when you get to heaven. However, we want to experience all of this that we can while still on the earth. The laying on of hands helps us to experience more of the heavenly on the earth now.

God wants us to have holy hands. Holy hands are hands that are an extension of a heart of love. Holy hands are hands that are motivated by love for God and love for others. We can lift holy hands to God if they are motivated by love, then we can use them for His glory. By laying hands on others, we can grow in Christ when we see how He loves to use us to bless others. It builds our faith in His love for them and for us.

When others lay hands on us, it can help our growth in Jesus, which is the basic desire of all true Christians— to grow in Christ.

Now What?

Father, I thank You for Your Son's nail-scarred hands. For I can see Your love for me through Your Son's hands. Use my hands to bless others even as You used Your Son's hands to bless and to destroy the works of the devil.

Holy Spirit, help me to grow in love so that my hands can truly bless others. Also, help me to receive the love others have for me through the laying on of their hands. In the name of the Nail-Scarred-One, I pray. Amen.

I desire therefore that the men pray everywhere, lifting up holy hands, without wrath and doubting.

1 Timothy 2:8

Chapter 10

Resurrection

*I*t is the greatest knowledge; it is the worst knowledge. It is the most wonderful news; it is the most horrible news. What is? The answer to a simple question that every human being faces: "What will happen to me when I die?"

All humans know that to be living means that death will come. Death is a part of life. All living things eventually die. All this death is the direct result of mankind's sin against God as Romans 5:12 says, *"Therefore, just as through one man sin entered the world, and death through sin, and thus death spread to all men, because all sinned"* (see also Genesis 2:17). Death came upon **all** living things because of sin as Romans 8:21 states, *"That the creation itself will be liberated from its bondage to decay and brought into the glorious freedom of the children of God"* (NIV).

Since death is all around us, it is easy to see that we will also die one day. However, our answer to the question asked above, "What will happen to me when I die?" determines our fear of death.

Some are afraid to die because they believe that death ends their existence. Indeed, if death is the end of existence, then who would want to die? Few, if any, would want to die, if in their right mind and not physically tormented, if death is the end of their existence. But death is not the end of a person's existence.

Others believe that they are reincarnated as another life form on earth after death. This may help some deal with the fear of death to a degree, but it is a lie. The truth is Hebrews 9:27: *"...man is destined to die once, and after that to face judgment"* (NIV). After *one* death is the judgment of God. This shows that there is an existence after death where God will pronounce a righteous judgment based upon whether you received Jesus Christ or not, and how you lived your life. There is no reincarnation. You only have *one chance* to live your life before you enter eternity.

The one belief we are interested in as a Christian is what Jesus believed and taught about life after death. He clearly answered the question, "Is there life after death?" He not only answered it, He became the answer. This brings us to the next basic principle of Christ in Hebrews 6:2—resurrection of the dead.

Resurrection of the dead is the central part of the good news (gospel). Without this part of the gospel, there is no good news. If death ends it all, we have no hope and no reason for faith. Again, we are faced with a most important question: "What will happen to me when I die?" Jesus answered this question for us, giving us a hope and faith in life after death. He did this in two basic ways: with His teachings and with His Resurrection. We will look at each of these individually, starting with His teachings.

His Teachings

Let's look at what Jesus said about life after death—what He taught. He said:

> He who believes in the Son has everlasting
> life; and he who does not believe the Son
> shall not see life, but the wrath of God abides
> on him. (John 3:36)

Through our faith in Christ, we have everlasting life. *Everlasting life* means that life goes on past death or it would not be everlasting life. This verse also shows that those that do not believe in Jesus are alive after death since the wrath of God *abides* on them.

When Jesus spoke about eternal life, He left no room for us to doubt what He believed. He emphasized the point that we have everlasting life when we believe in Him by saying, *"Most assuredly, I say to you."* Therefore, we should never doubt that we already have everlasting life when we believe in Him. Eternal life starts the moment we receive Jesus Christ as our Lord and Savior. We pass from eternal death into eternal life as soon as we are born again.

> Most assuredly, I say to you, he who hears
> My word and believes in Him who sent Me
> has everlasting life, and shall not come into
> judgment, but has passed from death into
> life. (John 5:24)

There are many Scriptures where Jesus speaks of eternal life. I will list a few more of them because your hope and expectancy for everlasting life increases when you hear or read the words of Jesus in relation to your life lasting forever.

> Most assuredly, I say to you, he who believes in Me has everlasting life. (John 6:47)

Eternal life is something you have when you are born again and no one can take it from you.

> My sheep hear My voice, and I know them, and they follow Me. And I give them eternal life, and they shall never perish; neither shall anyone snatch them out of My hand. (John 10:27–28)

Jesus' words in the next two verses show us that it is the Father's will for us to have everlasting life.

> And this is the will of Him who sent Me, that everyone who sees the Son and believes in Him may have everlasting life; and I will raise him up at the last day. (John 6:40)

> For God so loved the world that He gave His only begotten Son, that whoever believes in Him should not perish but have everlasting life. (John 3:16)

Jesus explains the purpose of everlasting life in John 17:3, "And this is eternal life, that they may know You, the only true God, and Jesus Christ whom You have sent."

Everlasting life is to know the Father and the Son. This experience will last forever. You will forever be learning about God, which is the most exciting thing possible. Just as the most important things in this life are the relationships you have with others, so the most important thing in eternity is to grow in your relationship with God.

Nothing is more exciting than being with the ones you love and learning about them. Yet, it will be even more exciting to be with the Creator of everything—including you—and to learn about Him for all eternity. Indeed, there will never be anything more fulfilling than to grow in your relationship with God—to grow in friendship and intimacy with Him. The closest thing we have on earth to compare it to is marriage. However, even the greatest marriage you can think of is only a shadow of the relationship God wants us to experience with Him forever. And it will take eternity to experience all of God. In fact, when you think it can't get any better, it will—forever, and forever, and forever.

> *But as it is written:*
>
> *"Eye has not seen, nor ear heard,*
> *Nor have entered into the heart of man*
> *The things which God has prepared for*
>   *those who love Him." (1 Corinthians 2:9)*

While we are experiencing everlasting life, those that do not have a relationship with Jesus will be experiencing everlasting death.

> *And these will go away into everlasting punishment, but the righteous into eternal life. (Matthew 25:46)*

Both life and death are everlasting. The righteous will experience everlasting life; those without Jesus will experience everlasting punishment. What is the worst punishment? It is separation from God. While eternal life is getting to know God, eternal death is not having that opportunity. Those that refused a relationship with Jesus while alive on earth will experience the ultimate horror—never, ever getting to have a relationship with God. Their eternal relationship will be with death and destruction. Their worst hell will be missing out on experiencing the love of God in a personal relationship.

As previously stated, Jesus came giving us a hope and faith in life after death—a resurrection of the dead. He did this in two basic ways. We have looked at the first way He did this—by His teachings. We will see now the second way He gives us a hope and faith in life after death—with His resurrection.

His Resurrection

The Gospel is JESUS *and the* RESURRECTION *of the dead.* Indeed, the gospel of the first century church was Jesus and the resurrection. Their message of Jesus and the resurrection of the dead through Him was easily discernible and that good news stirred up wrath and persecution.

> *Now as they spoke to the people, the priests, the captain of the temple, and the Sadducees came upon them, being greatly disturbed that they taught the people and preached in Jesus the resurrection from the dead. (Acts 4:1–2)*

*So they called them and commanded them
not to speak at all nor teach in the name of
Jesus. (Acts 4:18)*

Everyone wants to know what will happen to him or her after death. The early church made it so plain that they were forbidden to speak or teach in the name of Jesus (about Jesus' authority, especially over death). But God wants everyone to know that the resurrection from the dead is **in** Jesus.

The resurrection from the dead message is not just an "Easter Sunday message," but it is a vital part of the gospel. It should not be left out of it. This is an appropriate time to think about how often you have heard a message or sermon on the resurrection. Like most of us, it probably has been very seldom, if at all (not including Easter Sunday). When you leave out the resurrection, you are leaving out one of the most powerful parts of the gospel. Remember, resurrection is not just about Jesus being raised from the dead; it is about all of His people being raised from the grave. The early church knew that the resurrection of the dead through Jesus *is* the gospel. All resurrection life comes through the One (Jesus) who is resurrected from the dead.

Remember, eternal life and resurrection from the dead are not the same. You have eternal life when you believe; the resurrection of the dead is when your body is raised from the grave and reunited with your spirit.

I believe that before Jesus comes again to earth, this message of the resurrection of the dead will take its proper place in the gospel again. For Jesus said that He is the resurrection and the life (see John 11:25).

Jesus *is* the resurrection. He is the first person to be raised from the dead and to receive His glorified body. How do we know Jesus rose from the dead?

First, Jesus promised He would rise from the dead on the third day after His death.

> *For he was giving his disciples teaching, and saying to them, The Son of man is given up into the hands of men, and they will put him to death; and when he is dead, after three days he will come back from the dead. (Mark 9:31 BBE)*

Second, because the angel in the Bible tells us so:

> *But the angel answered and said to the women, "Do not be afraid, for I know that you seek Jesus who was crucified. He is not here; for He is risen . . ." (Matthew 28:5–6)*

Third, many people saw Jesus alive after His crucifixion.

> *. . . that he was buried; that he was raised from death on the third day, again exactly as Scripture says; that he presented himself alive to Peter, then to his closest followers, and later to more than five hundred of his followers all at the same time, most of them still around (although a few have since died); that he then spent time with James and the rest of those he commissioned to*

represent him; and that he finally presented himself alive to me. (1 Corinthians 15:4–8 TMSG)

Fourth, Thomas even put his finger in the nail prints in His hands (see John 20:26). Even so, Jesus would rather we believe He is risen from the dead without seeing Him as Thomas did. *"Jesus said to him, 'Thomas, because you have seen Me, you have believed. Blessed are those who have not seen and yet have believed'"* (John 20:29).

Furthermore, He does not like it when we do not believe the report of others that He is risen, that He is powerfully alive today—which means that He is able to do miracles through you!

> *Later He appeared to the eleven as they sat at the table; and He rebuked their unbelief and hardness of heart, because they did not believe those who had seen Him after He had risen. (Mark 16:14)*

The Good News is that He is alive—death could not hold Him. He tells us what happens to those that believe this wonderful news:

> *And these signs will follow those who believe: In My name they will cast out demons; they will speak with new tongues; they will take up serpents; and if they drink anything deadly, it will by no means hurt them; they will lay hands on the sick, and they will recover. (Mark 16:17–18)*

Importance of the Resurrection

The following Scripture shows the vital importance of the resurrection of the dead. If there is no resurrection then we have no hope.

> *For if the dead are not raised, then Christ has not been raised either. And if Christ has not been raised, your faith is futile; you are still in your sins! Then those also who have fallen asleep in Christ are lost. If only for this life we have hope in Christ, we are to be pitied more than all men. (1 Corinthians 15:16–19 NIV)*

This Scripture makes it clear that there is no gospel without the resurrection of the dead. However, the gospel is the good news that Jesus is resurrected from the dead, and in Him, we will also be raised from the grave.

> *For since death came through a man, the resurrection of the dead comes also through a man. For as in Adam all die, so in Christ all will be made alive. But each in his own turn: Christ, the firstfruits; then, when he comes, those who belong to him. (1 Corinthians 15:21–23 NIV)*

Notice when *"in Christ all will be made alive"* happens—it is *"when He comes."* Accordingly, these verses show us that those that have died do not yet have a physical body. Their physical body is in the grave and returns to dust (see Genesis 3:19). Their spirit has left their body and is either blessed or tormented. Jesus spoke about this in Luke 16:22–25:

> *Then he died, this poor man, and was taken up by the angels to the lap of Abraham. The rich man also died and was buried. In hell and in torment, he looked up and saw Abraham in the distance and Lazarus in his lap. He called out, "Father Abraham, mercy! Have mercy! Send Lazarus to dip his finger in water to cool my tongue. I'm in agony in this fire."*
>
> *But Abraham said, "Child, remember that in your lifetime you got the good things and Lazarus the bad things. It's not like that here. Here he's consoled and you're tormented."* (TMSG)

What Kind of Body Will We Have?

Even though the spirit leaves the body in death, the person still has a form that is recognizable as the person that they were on the earth. But they are not yet complete since God made us body, soul, and spirit. They are eagerly waiting for the resurrection of their bodies from the grave. So what kind of body will we have in the resurrection? We do not know exactly what we will be like except that we will be like Jesus.

> *Dear friends, we are already God's children, but he has not yet shown us what we will be like when Christ appears. But we do know that we will be like him . . . (1 John 3:2 NLT)*

We get a small picture of what we will be like when we see Jesus appearing after the resurrection in Luke 24:36–43:

> . . . Jesus Himself stood in the midst of them, and said . . . "Behold My hands and My feet, that it is I Myself. Handle Me and see, for a spirit does not have flesh and bones as you see I have."

> When He had said this, He showed them His hands and His feet. But while they still did not believe for joy, and marveled, He said to them, "Have you any food here?" So they gave Him a piece of a broiled fish and some honeycomb. And He took it and ate in their presence.

Also, the following verses will help to explain our new bodies:

> But someone will say, "How are the dead raised up? And with what body do they come?" Foolish one, what you sow is not made alive unless it dies. And what you sow, you do not sow that body that shall be, but mere grain—perhaps wheat or some other grain. But God gives it a body as He pleases, and to each seed its own body. . . . The body is sown in corruption, it is raised in incorruption. It is sown in dishonor, it is raised in glory. It is sown in weakness, it is raised in power. It is sown a natural body, it

is raised a spiritual body. There is a natural body, and there is a spiritual body. . . .

The first man was of the earth, made of dust; the second Man is the Lord from heaven. . . . And as we have borne the image of the man of dust, we shall also bear the image of the heavenly Man. . . .

Behold, I tell you a mystery: We shall not all sleep [die], but we shall all be changed—in a moment, in the twinkling of an eye, at the last trumpet. For the trumpet will sound, and the dead will be raised incorruptible, and we shall be changed. For this corruptible must put on incorruption, and this mortal must put on immortality. So when this corruptible has put on incorruption, and this mortal has put on immortality, then shall be brought to pass the saying that is written: "Death is swallowed up in victory."

"O Death, where is your sting? O Hades, where is your victory?" (1 Corinthians 15:35–55)

Some have misunderstood when *"Death is swallowed up in victory."* They think it is already accomplished. But according to the Scripture above, *"at the last trumpet . . . the dead will be raised incorruptible . . . then shall be brought to pass the saying that is written: 'Death is swallowed up in victory.'"*

When we misunderstand the timing of "death being swallowed up in victory," we weaken the gospel of the resurrection of the dead. For the resurrection of all the saints is when death is swallowed up in victory and death loses its entire sting. Yes, the *fear* of death is defeated already because of Jesus' resurrection, but the *sting* of death is still here. We know this to be true because when a loved one dies, it stings. Why? Because they are not with us any longer. But when the last trump sounds and all are raised from the dead with incorruptible bodies and those alive at that time will also receive incorruptible bodies, being together at last, the sting of death is gone! Why? Because the sting of death comes from being separated from our loved ones, and from waiting for our glorified body.

Jesus' resurrection is the victory over death and that victory will be completed when we also have our resurrected bodies. Even so, there is a further implementation of that victory when we raise the dead as Jesus commanded us to do. *"And as you go, preach, saying, 'The kingdom of heaven is at hand.' Heal the sick, cleanse the lepers, raise the dead, cast out demons. Freely you have received, freely give"* (Matthew 10:7–8).

Because of Jesus' resurrection from the dead, we have the right and the commissions to raise the dead, heal the sick, cleanse the lepers, and cast out demons. As Acts 26:8 states, *"Why should it be thought incredible by you that God raises the dead?"* However, we may have to get over what other people think of us praying, especially for the dead, before we can release life as Jesus did when He raised a girl from the dead in Luke 8:52–55:

> *Now all wept and mourned for her; but He said, "Do not weep; she is not dead, but sleeping." And they ridiculed Him, knowing that she was dead.*
>
> *But He put them all outside, took her by the hand and called, saying, "Little girl, arise." Then her spirit returned, and she arose immediately.*

Because Jesus is the resurrection of life, we can raise the dead in His name (His authority)—which means we can do it only as He directs us to. Jesus only raised the dead as the Father directed Him to since He was under the Father's authority. Being under Jesus' authority, we too will raise the dead ones that He directs us to raise.

Raising the dead in Jesus' name proves that Jesus was raised from the dead Himself. How? It shows His power over death because death could not hold Him— He broke its power. Because of His resurrection, we are to make disciples of all nations since He now has *all* authority in heaven and earth.

> *And Jesus came and spoke to them, saying, "All authority has been given to Me in heaven and on earth. Go therefore and make disciples of all the nations . . ." (Matthew 28:18–19)*

When Will We Be Raised

Jesus is the resurrection that all believers will experience, but when will this happen? It will happen at God's command when Jesus returns to earth:

> *And regarding the question, friends, that has come up about what happens to those already dead and buried, we don't want you in the dark any longer. . . . God will most certainly bring back to life those who died in Jesus.*
>
> *. . . when the Master comes again to get us, those of us who are still alive will not get a jump on the dead and leave them behind. In actual fact, they'll be ahead of us. The Master himself will give the command. Archangel thunder! God's trumpet blast! He'll come down from heaven and the dead in Christ will rise—they'll go first. Then the rest of us who are still alive at the time will be caught up with them into the clouds to meet the Master. (1 Thessalonians 4:13–17 TMSG)*

Our Gain

We brought nothing into this world and we can take nothing out of it. Jesus set the example for us—the King of the universe came into the world with *nothing*. He came as a baby with all the needs of a child. Then when He left this world, He was completely naked on a cross. He took nothing with Him. So what can we gain while on earth?

Now godliness with contentment is great gain. For we brought nothing into this world, and it is certain we can carry nothing out. And having food and clothing, with these we shall be content. (1 Timothy 6:6–8)

Godliness with contentment is what we can gain while on earth.

The Cross

On the cross, Jesus was in the middle of two thieves, one on His right, and one on His left. One believed in *Jesus on the cross*, the other did not believe. One went to be with Jesus, the other did not.

Your eternal inheritance is on the other side of death with the cross as the dividing line of your inheritance. If you believe in Jesus—what He did for you on the cross—then you will be with Him forever. If you do not believe in Jesus and His sacrificial death for you, you will not be with Him after death.

Surely, the day that looked like the greatest defeat, the cross, was the day of the greatest victory. So also is your death as a Christian; it is your greatest moment of life!

Precious in the sight of the Lord
Is the death of His saints.

Psalm 116:15

Now What?

Heavenly Father, I thank You for the eternal life that I now have through Jesus. Jesus, I thank You for dying for me so that I may live, and for taking away the fear of death. Thank You for all of my loved ones that have received You and have eternal life. Even so, I pray for those that still do not know You that before they die, they will pass from death into life through You.

Holy Spirit, help me to know the power of Jesus' resurrection and to be a witness to it. For I want to see the power of His resurrection released through me so others may know that they can have eternal life in Christ. And that I would give hope and faith in the resurrection of our bodies from the grave. In Your name I pray. Amen.

He who has the Son has life; he who does not have the Son of God does not have life. These things I have written to you who believe in the name of the Son of God, that you may know that you have eternal life...

1 John 5:12–13

Chapter 11

Judgment

*T*he next basic principle of Christ in Hebrews 6:2 is *eternal judgment*. This judgment is a judgment that lasts forever. This does not mean that the process of judgment lasts forever but that the result of the judgment lasts forever. When many of us think of God's judgment, we only think of it as condemnation or punishment. However, this judgment sets our eternal destiny as a born-again Christian—being with God forever.

The Scriptures exalt God's judgments as something *greatly* to be desired. *"The judgments of the LORD are true and righteous altogether. More to be desired are they than gold, Yea, than much fine gold; Sweeter also than honey and the honeycomb"* (Psalm 19:9–10).

As a Christian, we should especially welcome His *eternal* judgment. Why? Let me list three reasons: First, as the above verse states, His judgments are true and righteous altogether. Second, as we also mentioned, this judgment sets our eternal destiny—being with God forever. Third, we should welcome His eternal judgment because the One who loves us more than anyone is our Judge. *". . . [Jesus] was ordained by God to be Judge of the living and the dead"* (Acts 10:42). We can take comfort in the fact that our Judge, Jesus, loves us perfectly. Even so, His eternal judgments can be horrifying since they establish the eternal state of both the righteous and the wicked. His eternal judgments are wonderful for the righteous, but are horrifying for the unrighteous.

> *He who is unjust, let him be unjust still; he who is filthy, let him be filthy still; he who is righteous, let him be righteous still; he who is holy, let him be holy still. (Revelation 22:11)*

Eternal judgment for the Christian is God rewarding us for believing in His Son and for our works. This judgment is not just based upon what we did, but *why* we did it. This judgment is based upon keeping the two great commandments—loving God and loving others. To the degree we have kept these two commandments through learning to love, we will be rewarded. These rewards will be for doing what Jesus wanted us to do with our lives—loving God first, and then loving others. As 1 Corinthians 13:1–3 informs us, only things done through love will profit us anything. For our actions are counted as nothing if they are not based upon love. The things done without love will be burned up (see 1 Corinthians 3:11–15).

Eternal judgment for a born-again Christian is not about salvation, but about rewards. As the last chapter showed, you have eternal life the moment you receive Jesus Christ as your Lord. Even so, we shall all stand before the judgment seat of Christ to give an account of our life. *"For we must all appear before the judgment seat of Christ, that each one may receive the things done in the body, according to what he has done, whether good or bad"* (2 Corinthians 5:9–10).

Boldness in the Day of Judgment

If you want to have boldness on the Day of Judgment, it only comes one way. Boldness comes by knowing and believing in the love that God has for you. Then from abiding in that love, you live a life of loving God and others, which will cast out the fear of judgment.

> *And we have known and believed the love that God has for us. God is love, and he who abides in love abides in God, and God in him.*

> *Love has been perfected among us in this: that we may have boldness in the day of judgment; because as He is, so are we in this world. There is no fear in love; but perfect love casts out fear, because fear involves torment. But he who fears has not been made perfect in love. (1 John 4:16–18)*

The Second Death

We all need to know that the Scriptures speak of a *second* death, and that God does not want us to be a part of it. The second death is the worst death possible since it is spiritual and eternal. It is eternal separation from God in the lake of fire. The only way to escape the second death is to have our names written in the Book of Life. *"The lake of fire is the second death. If anyone's*

name was not found written in the book of life, he was
thrown into the lake of fire" (Revelation 20:14–15 NIV).

The Final Judgment

The final judgment mentioned above in Revelation
20 takes place after the first resurrection. If we are a
part of the first resurrection, then the second death has
no power over us. Plus, those that are part of the first
resurrection will reign with Christ for one thousand
years.

> *Blessed and holy are those who have part in*
> *the first resurrection. The second death has*
> *no power over them, but they will be priests*
> *of God and of Christ and will reign with him*
> *for a thousand years. (Revelation 20:6 NIV)*

If we are already free from sin in Christ, then our
physical death releases us to total freedom in Him.
However, if a person is bound in sin, not knowing Jesus
as Savior, then that person will have a first death *and* a
second death—experiencing total bondage and eternal
dying. They will experience the worst possible thing—
the separation from God's presence for all of eternity.

This is one of the basic principles of Christ—eternal
judgment—and a basic part of the gospel. Remember,
the *entire* gospel is good news. This includes the
Scriptures that describe the ends of the righteous and
the unrighteous. Yes, the news that the unrighteous are
cast into the lake of fire is good news (although not for
them) because if everyone is treated the same no matter
what they did with their life, then righteousness would
have no meaning or value. The good news is that Jesus

makes a distinction between the righteous and the unrighteous. Since God makes such a serious distinction between those that do right and those that do wrong, it magnifies the value of doing what pleases God. Eternal judgment is good news because all of our God-pleasing works carry great value, which we will be rewarded for.

The *focus* of our life should be to become like Jesus. The central characteristic of Jesus is love. If we have learned to love then we will be bearing His image, for God is love. This is what He will be looking for when He judges us—our love for Him and our love for others. All of our works will be judged by this.

The Bible encourages us to live totally in Christ now so that we are not ashamed when He appears, but confident in our relationship with Him as our Lord.

> *And now, children, stay with Christ. Live deeply in Christ. Then we'll be ready for him when he appears, ready to receive him with open arms, with no cause for red-faced guilt or lame excuses when he arrives. (1 John 2:28 TMSG)*

As stated earlier, the judgments of God are desirable; they are an invitation to do what is right. An example of this is when Jesus spoke to the churches in Revelation chapters 2 and 3, He promised rewards if they would respond to His judgments. His judgments were for the good of every person in each of those churches. Without Jesus judging what was right and wrong in their lives, they would not have known what to keep on doing and what to stop doing. But through Jesus' judgments, they knew what to do and what the rewards were for obeying His judgments. So it is with us, God gives direction to our lives through His judgments of what we are doing right and wrong. Then He invites us to do what is right, plus, offers us rewards for doing right.

When we know that we will all face the eternal judgment of Christ, it establishes boundaries in our life. We will want to live a life pleasing to the One who is our Judge. We will want to obey Him, especially His commands to love. For it is very sobering to know that this life establishes our eternal destiny. Many have not realized that not everyone is equal in heaven. Everyone is in God's presence and in eternal bliss, but not everyone is the same. The disciples of Jesus argued over who would be the greatest in heaven because they knew some would be closer to God than others would be. They even asked Jesus to let them sit on His right and left hand.

> *So He said to them, ". . . to sit on My right hand and on My left is not Mine to give, but it is for those for whom it is prepared by My Father."*
>
> *". . . but whoever desires to become great among you, let him be your servant. And whoever desires to be first among you, let him be your slave—just as the Son of Man did not come to be served, but to serve, and to give His life a ransom for many."* (Matthew 20:23–28)

I believe that Jesus is saying that to be great you must be like Him and the more you are like Him, the more you will serve God and others in love. In view of that, I believe that the closer you are to fully loving God and others on earth, the closer you will be to Him in heaven. In other words, the more you keep the two greatest commandments, the greater you will be throughout eternity.

Your goal should not be greatness in the sight of men, but greatness in the sight of God. To be great in the sight of God is to be like His Son Jesus. Jesus served God and humanity in His life and is the greatest in heaven.

What Should We Do?

As a newborn Christian, you are like a little child wanting to learn everything you can. Don't ever lose this because childlikeness is precious to God. Little children are not full of themselves, but are full of wonder. They want to grow and mature. So if you want to grow in Jesus, become as a little child.

> *At that time the disciples came to Jesus, saying, "Who then is greatest in the kingdom of heaven?"*
>
> *Then Jesus called a little child to Him, set him in the midst of them, and said, "Assuredly, I say to you, unless you are converted and become as little children, you will by no means enter the kingdom of heaven. Therefore whoever humbles himself*

as this little child is the greatest in the
kingdom of heaven." (Matthew 18:1–4)

Our short lives prepare us for eternity. Because of this, we need to make every day count. We need God to teach us how to live well.

We live for seventy years or so (with luck
we might make it to eighty),
And what do we have to show for it?

. . . Oh! Teach us to live well!
Teach us to live wisely and well!
(Psalm 90:10–12 TMSG)

Conclusion to—Growth: The Basics

This concludes the second section of this book—Growth: The Basics. The reason we covered all of these basics is for your growth in Christ. These basics, along with the first section of this book—Growth: The Foundation, give you a solid base to grow on. I believe your future growth will be based upon the truths covered in the first two sections of this book.

As you read the Bible, you will find several passages that invite you to grow in Christ. In fact, it shows that growth in Christ is the most important thing in life. The following is the passage I based this section of the book on, which encourages you to grow up in Christ.

. . . Grow up in Christ. The basic
foundational truths are in place: turning
your back on "salvation by self-help" and
turning in trust toward God; baptismal

instructions; laying on of hands; resurrection of the dead; eternal judgment. God helping us, we'll stay true to all that. But there's so much more. Let's get on with it! (Hebrews 6:1–3 TMSG)

We are invited to grow up—to attain full growth in Christ.

Now What?

My Father, I know that Your judgments are pure and right. I know that one day I will stand before Christ to give an account of how I lived. I have peace about that Day, but not total peace because of the hardness of my heart. For I have not yet learned to love as I should. Holy Spirit, in the name of Jesus, help me to grow in love, to love You more and to love others more. Because I do not want to stand before Jesus with regrets about not growing in love. Amen.

God wants us to grow up, to know the whole truth and tell it in love—like Christ in everything. We take our lead from Christ, who is the source of everything we do.

Ephesians 4:15 TMSG

Growth:

THE

FINISH

Chapter 12

His Body

*B*efore we begin the third section of this book, Growth: THE FINISH, we need to realize that this section of the book may be harder to "chew" than the previous sections. We now want to introduce "solid food." The Scriptures speak of the basics of growth in Christ as *milk*. Then as we grow in Christ beyond just the basics, we are to receive more and more *solid food*. The foundational Scripture we are using for this book explains it this way (for those who have not just recently been born again):

> *You have been believers so long now that you ought to be teaching others. Instead, you need someone to teach you again the basic things about God's word. You are like babies who need milk and cannot eat solid food. For someone who lives on milk is still an infant and doesn't know how to do what is right. Solid food is for those who are mature, who through training have the skill to recognize the difference between right and wrong.*

> *So let us stop going over the basic teachings about Christ again and again. Let us go on instead and become mature in our understanding. Surely we don't need to start*

again with the fundamental importance of repenting from evil deeds and placing our faith in God. You don't need further instruction about baptisms, the laying on of hands, the resurrection of the dead, and eternal judgment. And so, God willing, we will move forward to further understanding.
(Hebrews 5:12–6:3 NLT)

With these things in mind, we will now begin section three of this book.

There are three necessities for growth based upon the foundation and the basics that were covered thus far. It is assumed, as a Christian, that you are doing these three necessary things. The three obvious things for your growth in Christ are: prayer, Bible study, and fellowship with others.

Prayer is for building a personal relationship with the Father, Son, and Holy Spirit. This is a major key for your growth in Jesus. For without a personal relationship with God, how can you grow in Him? Certainly, your growth in Him is directly related to your relationship with Him. If you do not want to pursue a personal relationship with God, your growth will be limited to an *outward show* instead of a true *inward growth* by the Holy Spirit.

Of course, the key issue here is time. Some have said that our time is the most valuable thing we can give or withhold. As with all relationships, a relationship with God requires time. The more time spent with God, the greater the relationship will be. If we say we don't have time to pray, we are saying we don't have time for God.

Although we may not say it directly, to not spend time with God is saying, "I do not have time for You," with our actions. Most of us, if not all of us, have been guilty of this.

You cannot grow in Christ without spending time with Him. By His Spirit, He is continually inviting you to spend time with Him. If you will respond, God will "multiply" all your other time so that you will be able to do more than you thought possible.

Bible study is for teaching, training, guidance, education in righteousness—so you may be complete, ready for every good work (see 2 Timothy 3:16–17). Just by stating the purpose of Bible reading and study, it is apparent that this is another major key for your growth in Christ. In fact, it seems from 2 Timothy 3:16–17, that you will not be complete and thoroughly equipped for every good work without the Scriptures.

Keep in mind that when you read the Bible you are reading the very words of the Holy Spirit. Because of this, you can develop a very personal relationship with Him. For when you read the Bible as a personal book written to you, it will revolutionize your life. You will begin more and more to think as the Holy Spirit thinks. Then you will begin to act more and more like Him. This is true holiness—the Holy Spirit's life lived in you.

Fellowship with others is ideal for your inward growth. For sure, all your relationships will test your growth in Christ. Without these relationships, you cannot mature as you should. Family life and church life will give you opportunities to grow in love—which is your most important growth. Many run from these two (family life and church life) and miss their love-growth potential.

Certainly, this key to growth (fellowship with others) is dependent upon the first two keys to our growth. This "fellowship key" for our growth needs the first key (our relationship to God through *prayer*) to relate properly to and function in the family and church. Additionally, the "fellowship key" needs the *Bible's* teachings to know the proper way to get along with others. Indeed, much of the Scriptures deal with our relationships with one another and we can save ourselves a lot of heartache by knowing the Biblical truths concerning relationships.

Many have been hurt by the church (the body of Christ). In like manner, their own physical body has hurt many. Even so, when a part of our physical body hurts us, we try to heal the hurt. We don't think about leaving our body because it hurt us. We try everything to fix the hurt. We may even call in or go to a professional to get the hurt healed. Why do we do this? Because our body is a part of us. So it is the same with the church, we are baptized into the body of Christ. Jesus places us into a body of believers by His Spirit. *"But now God has set the members, each one of them, in the body just as He pleased"* (1 Corinthians 12:18).

God is the author of relationships. He established the relationship to Himself as primary and the relationship to others next. These two relationships are keys to our growth. Without both of these relationships, life will never be fulfilling as God intended. For we are made to be a part of the body of Christ because of our relationship to Him. When we resist either one of these, we are resisting the very thing that will propel us to our destiny.

Get over any hurts you have toward God or others and let the healing take place so that you can have healthy growth. God established healthy growth for your physical body as well as healthy growth in the body of Christ (the church). It is interesting that Jesus said, *"You must be born again"* (see John 3:7). Just as a newborn child needs others to grow, so you too as a born-again Christian need others in order to grow.

How much do we need others for our growth? 1 Corinthians chapter 12 and Ephesians chapter 4 are two excellent places that answer some of that question. The rest of the answer is in the remaining Scriptures. I can summarize the answer with the fact that when a person's spirit leaves their body they cease to grow. We call it death. So it is with a Christian whose spirit (heart) has left the body of Christ (the church). They cease to grow.

The Bible *stresses* the importance of the body of Christ. In fact, it plainly informs us of why many Christians are weak, sick, and even die before their time. Christians whose *heart* has left the body of Christ not only cease to grow, but may become weak, sick, and may die prematurely according to 1 Corinthians 11:29–30:

> . . . *not discerning the Lord's body. For this reason many are weak and sick among you, and many sleep [die prematurely].*

To discern the Lord's body is to recognize that He is the Head and we are a part of His body. We cannot separate ourselves from the Head without serious consequences. In like manner, we cannot separate ourselves from the rest of the body of Christ without consequences. And 1 Corinthians 11 lists some of the possible consequences of not discerning the Lord's body (the church). Why? Because we are baptized into the church—we are an essential part of the body of Christ. It is to our benefit to recognize this baptism and to surrender fully to it.

The Scriptures are very plain about our growth taking place within the body of Christ. In fact, this is what most of the New Testament epistles deal with—growing together in Christ.

> *I have a serious concern to bring up with you, my friends, using the authority of Jesus, our Master. I'll put it as urgently as I can: You must get along with each other. You must learn to be considerate of one another, cultivating a life in common. (1 Corinthians 1:10 TMSG)*

The Scripture does not baby us when it comes to being a part of the church and getting along with each other, but gives us solid food.

> *Brothers, I could not address you as spiritual but as worldly—mere infants in Christ. I gave you milk, not solid food, for you were not yet ready for it. Indeed, you are still not ready. You are still worldly. For since there is jealousy and quarreling among you, are*

*you not worldly? Are you not acting like
mere men? (1 Corinthians 3:1–3 NIV)*

*I, therefore, the prisoner of the Lord, beseech
you to walk worthy of the calling with which
you were called, with all lowliness and
gentleness, with longsuffering, bearing with
one another in love, endeavoring to keep the
unity of the Spirit in the bond of peace.
(Ephesians 4:1–3)*

Just as we want our children to get along with each
other, so God wants His children to get along with one
another. In fact, we find that a good portion of Jesus'
"last prayer" before going to the cross was about all of us
becoming one. This is not just a superficial unity but a
complete unity, a unity that will impact the world with
the love of God. Furthermore, this unity is to be so
strong that we become one as God is one—to have the
same unity the Father has with the Son. This is
something Jesus prayed for, which will be answered by
the Father.

*My prayer is not for them alone. I pray also
for those who will believe in me through
their message, that all of them may be one,
Father, just as you are in me and I am in
you. May they also be in us so that the world
may believe that you have sent me. I have
given them the glory that you gave me, that
they may be one as we are one: I in them
and you in me. May they be brought to
complete unity to let the world know that*

you sent me and have loved them even as
you have loved me. (John 17:20–23 NIV)

To have the unity Jesus desires, we must have a proper birth. The proper birth is a head-first birth. This is when the body follows the birthing of the head. A breach birth is when the body is birthed first and the head follows. Too many born-again Christians act as if they had a "breach birth." They do things their own way and then expect Jesus to bless them. They may or may not become a member of a local church, and if they do, they look for a church that agrees with them, one that will give them the growth they want to experience.

In contrast, many born-again Christians obviously had a "head-first birth." They *"follow the lamb (Jesus) wherever He goes"* (see Revelation 14:4–5). They ask God to send them to the church He wants them to be a part of—where they may grow however He wants them to grow. Then they become a vital member of that church.

I believe that generally my life has looked like a "head-first birth." However, there is some hesitation in proclaiming this because I can remember too many times in my life where I chose my way over His way (and at times, still do). I have no excuse because my life is based upon the proper foundation, Jesus (section one of this book), and I know and normally practice the basics (section two of this book). I have the power of the Holy Spirit to be a witness to Jesus—for my life to be a testimony of Jesus as Head of the body. Yet, too often, I have lived otherwise. But having the baptism of the Holy

Spirit leaves me without excuse for I have the power of
the Spirit to live as a testimony to Jesus.

*But you shall receive power when the Holy
Spirit has come upon you; and you shall be
witnesses to Me . . . (Acts 1:8)*

I am so glad that God looks at the heart. He knows
that my heart is to follow Him as the Head of the church
even when my actions seem to indicate otherwise. Even
so, when I sin (miss the mark), I need to confess the sin
and turn from it (see 1 John 1:9).

Before we move on, let me mention one more thing
about prayer, Bible study, and fellowship with others. I
do not believe it is about doing more, but about
experiencing more. I think God is more concerned about
your heart than your actions. I believe it is not about
how much time you pray, it is about how much you *love*
to pray to the Father. The same is true of Bible study.
For it is not about how much you study, but about how
much you *love* to study about God. Finally, it is not
about how much you fellowship with others, it is about
how much you *love* to fellowship with others. If love of
God and others is not motivating you to do more, doing
more will not profit you. Even so, the more you love
these things, the more you will do them.

The Head

The head is where most of the interaction with the
world takes place. We see, hear, smell, taste, and speak
from the head. We spend the most time grooming the
head since it is the most presentable part of the body. As

a Christian, our Head, Jesus, is the most presentable part of us. We are to lift up our Head (Jesus) by seeing with His eyes, hearing with His ears, smelling (discerning) with His nose, and speaking with His mouth. How do we do these things? By His Holy Spirit:

> *Or do you not know that your body is the temple of the Holy Spirit who is in you, whom you have from God, and you are not your own? For you were bought at a price; therefore glorify God in your body and in your spirit, which are God's. (1 Corinthians 6:19–20)*

The three keys we have been writing about come into play here again: prayer, Bible study, and fellowship with others. These three things will help us to see, hear, discern, and speak as Jesus would. They will help us to abide in Him. By abiding in Him, we will bear much fruit (growth).

> *I am the vine, you are the branches. He who abides in Me, and I in him, bears much fruit; for without Me you can do nothing. If anyone does not abide in Me, he is cast out as a branch and is withered; and they gather them and throw them into the fire, and they are burned. (John 15:5–6)*

Jesus' disciples bear much fruit because they abide in Him. If anyone does not abide in Him, they are in serious trouble according to His warning above. Because

He loves us, He warns us straightforwardly—He must be our Head or we will not grow; we will wither.

Jesus desires for us to be His disciple. A disciple is a disciplined follower of Christ, the Head. And the main reason one would be His disciple is to be like Him, which brings the Father the most glory. For the greatest fruit you can bear is to be like His Son. The more you are like Jesus; the more the Father is glorified.

The Body

Where can we best follow the Head? It is in the body of Christ—for He is the Head of the body. *"And He is the head of the body, the church, who is the beginning, the firstborn from the dead, that in all things He may have the preeminence"* (Colossians 1:18). Jesus is to have first place in all things.

The body of Christ is the place for our growth, and the Head of the body gives gifts to the body for that growth. If we want to grow, the best place to be is in the body of Christ.

> *. . . And He Himself gave some to be apostles, some prophets, some evangelists, and some pastors and teachers, for the equipping of the saints for the work of ministry, for the edifying of the body of Christ, till we all come to the unity of the faith and of the knowledge of the Son of God, to a perfect man, to the measure of the stature of the fullness of Christ . . . (Ephesians 4:11–13)*

These verses speak about growing *"to the measure of the stature of the fullness of Christ,"* which is the basis of this book. Furthermore, these verses show again that we cannot properly grow apart from the body of Christ. For these verses go on to say:

> *. . . but, speaking the truth in love, may grow up in all things into Him who is the head—Christ—from whom the whole body, joined and knit together by what every joint supplies, according to the effective working by which every part does its share, causes growth of the body for the edifying of itself in love. (Ephesians 4:15–16)*

It takes every part of the body of Christ for us to grow as we should, especially in the area of love.

We also want to point out the specific gifts He gave to men for our growth. *"He Himself gave some to be apostles, some prophets, some evangelists, and some pastors and teachers"* (Ephesians 4:11). Why did He give these gifts? He gave these gifts for all of us to, *"come to the unity of the faith and of the knowledge of the Son of God, to a perfect man, to the measure of the stature of the fullness of Christ"* (Ephesians 4:13).

We need to partake of the five ministry giftings that Jesus gave to His body. For the evangelist makes the compassion of Jesus come alive in us. The pastor makes relationships come alive. The teacher makes the Word of God come alive. The prophet makes the voice of the Lord come alive. The apostle makes the desire for Christ to be formed in us to come alive.

God's goal for us is to become *"a perfect man, to the measure of the stature of the fullness of Christ."* No, you cannot do this on your own because the vehicle God designed for this is the body of Christ. Jesus is the Head of the *body,* which you are designed to be part of.

Now What?

Father, I thank You for baptizing me into the body of Christ. Show me anywhere I may be offended with anyone and help me to turn from it. Help me never to allow offense to take root in my heart.

Holy Spirit, teach me to love the whole body of Christ, as well as, my local church. Help me to be the blessing You have called me to be for the body of Christ. In Jesus' name I pray. Amen.

For by one Spirit we were all baptized into one body whether Jews or Greeks, whether slaves or free—and have all been made to drink into one Spirit. For in fact the body is not one member but many.

1 Corinthians 12:13–14

Chapter 13

His Disciple

I cannot be His disciple unless there is a hunger for it. Hunger, like all things for the Christian, begins with God. We desire Him because He first desired us. Out of His desire for us, our desire for Him is birthed. This is what attracted the first disciples of Jesus. Jesus would say to them, *"Follow Me."* As they responded to Jesus' desire for them, a desire for Him was birthed.

All true discipleship starts with knowing God's desire for you. When the Holy Spirit speaks to your heart to follow Him, you do not just hear words; you feel His desire for a personal walk with you. The deeper you feel His desire for you, the deeper your desire to follow Him will be. As stated, discipleship begins with hunger. This hunger begins when you start to understand the extreme love God has for you.

This hunger seeks to be fulfilled and the way of fulfillment is through being a disciple. A disciple is a disciplined follower of Jesus. The motivation for this disciplined life is our love for Him. Consequently, our discipleship will never go higher than the measure of our love for Him. For our love for Him is the greatest motivator of our actions.

Being a follower of someone is not strange because we all follow someone. Some follow themselves—what they think and believe. Others mostly follow a relative, a friend, or a special person they admire.

The greatest person you could ever follow is Jesus. When you are His disciple, it is all about a relationship with Him. If your motivation for being a disciple is not a relationship with Jesus, then it is not true discipleship. Even though we are created for a deep relationship with Him (discipleship), many do not grow in this.

You should hear the call to discipleship as an invitation to friendship. God is asking to be your friend. He wants you! Imagine, the God of all creation, the One beyond everyone and everything, desires you—your friendship, not just a casual friendship, but a most intimate friendship. This friendship with God is made available through Jesus Christ.

The Word (Jesus) became flesh and dwelt among us so we could behold Him and have a deep relationship with Him. We are created to behold Him—how He lived, what He taught. *"And the Word became flesh and dwelt among us, and we beheld His glory, the glory as of the only begotten of the Father, full of grace and truth"* (John 1:14).

Heartfelt Words

Jesus is the master of birthing disciples. Let's see how He birthed His first disciples. In doing this, we will unlock the basis of discipleship. Jesus first called four fishermen:

> *And Jesus, walking by the Sea of Galilee,*
> *saw two brothers, Simon called Peter, and*

Andrew his brother, casting a net into the sea; for they were fishermen. Then He said to them, "Follow Me, and I will make you fishers of men." They immediately left their nets and followed Him.

Going on from there, He saw two other brothers, James the son of Zebedee, and John his brother, in the boat with Zebedee their father, mending their nets. He called them, and immediately they left the boat and their father, and followed Him. (Matthew 4:18–22)

Wow! Whatever Jesus did caused these four men to immediately leave everything and follow Him. So what did He do that caused such a reaction? He revealed His heart for these men. They did not just hear the words, *"Follow Me,"* they heard the heart of Jesus in those words. They felt the call of God for intimacy with them deeply in their hearts. They felt His desire for them. This sparked a like response in their hearts. They immediately wanted to follow Him, and they did.

Another reason that they immediately left everything to follow Him was because He gave them a destiny—something to do. His destiny for their life was greater than they imagined, but if they followed Him, He promised to bring them into it. This sparked the desire in them to leave everything to obtain the destiny He promised them.

From reading the above passage of Scripture, you may think that they had no previous knowledge of Jesus or His teachings. So let us look at a parallel passage from Luke 5:1–11 that may show otherwise:

> *Once when he was standing on the shore of Lake Gennesaret [Sea of Galilee], the crowd was pushing in on him to better hear the Word of God. He noticed two boats tied up. The fishermen had just left them and were out scrubbing their nets. He climbed into the boat that was Simon's and asked him to put out a little from the shore. Sitting there, using the boat for a pulpit, he taught the crowd.*
>
> *When he finished teaching, he said to Simon, "Push out into deep water and let your nets out for a catch."*
>
> *. . . It was no sooner said than done—a huge haul of fish, straining the nets past capacity. They waved to their partners in the other boat to come help them. They filled both boats, nearly swamping them with the catch.*
>
> *Simon Peter, when he saw it, fell to his knees before Jesus. "Master, leave. I'm a sinner and can't handle this holiness. Leave me to myself." When they pulled in that catch of fish, awe overwhelmed Simon and everyone with him. It was the same with James and John, Zebedee's sons, coworkers with Simon.*
>
> *Jesus said to Simon, "There is nothing to fear. From now on you'll be fishing for men and women." They pulled their boats up on*

the beach, left them, nets and all, and followed him. (TMSG)

We see from this passage of Scripture that they probably knew Jesus but felt like they were not worthy to follow Him. However, when they heard Jesus' call to their hearts, it disarmed their fears. The key to discipleship is hearing God's call—His desire and invitation for deep intimacy with you even if you feel unworthy to follow Him. Then when you think it is too good to be true, He reveals your destiny to you—if you will follow Him. No, you will not feel worthy of the destiny He has for you—the things He wants you to be and do. But that is why it is called *grace*—the unmerited favor and power to be and to do all He has called you to.

"Follow Me" is a call to intimacy. Discipleship is about intimacy. Intimacy is about love. Hearing God's call of love is hearing His call to discipleship—intimacy. The deeper you hear His call of love, the deeper your discipleship can be.

God's call of love is perceived best at the cross (see John 3:16). The cross is the beginning place of discipleship. For at the cross, God's overwhelming desire for intimacy with you is revealed. He wants intimacy with you so much that He paid the greatest price possible—His Son.

As for my life, I need more comprehension of His love for me because I do not consider myself a very disciplined follower. Even so, I *want* to be a more disciplined follower, therefore I meditate often on His love for me. For I know that love is the greatest motivating force—along with my destiny (the reason I was created to live on the earth at this time). Part of my destiny is to write books that will help others. I do not feel worthy to do this, but by His grace, I write.

When you are in love, a disciplined life is much easier. I remember what happened to me when I first fell in love with my wife. My life became quite disciplined so that I could spend as much time with her as possible. Love can cause anyone to become more disciplined so that he or she can have more time for intimacy with the one who is loved. Again, discipleship is about intimacy with the One you love. Even more than that, it is about the One who loves intimacy with you!

Requirements for Discipleship

The first requirement for discipleship is that you must be born again. Some equate discipleship with salvation. I do not. I believe you may be saved while not being much of a disciple. Nevertheless, your life will not be all God desires for it to be and you will suffer loss for not following Him as you should. I base my belief upon all we have covered thus far in this book including 1 Corinthians 3:11–15:

> *For no other foundation can anyone lay than that which is laid, which is Jesus Christ. Now if anyone builds on this foundation with gold, silver, precious stones, wood, hay, straw, each one's work will become clear; for the Day will declare it, because it will be revealed by fire; and the fire will test each one's work, of what sort it is. If anyone's*

*work which he has built on it endures, he will
receive a reward. If anyone's work is burned,
he will suffer loss; but he himself will be
saved, yet so as through fire.*

Our lives are to be built upon the foundation, which
is Jesus Christ. The things built upon following Jesus
(discipleship) will endure. The things not built upon
discipleship (not following Jesus) will be destroyed.
Even so, *"If anyone's work is burned, he will suffer loss;
but he himself will be saved, yet so as through fire"*
(1 Corinthians 3:15).

Furthermore, I believe you may be saved while not
being much of a disciple because Jesus said you have
eternal life the moment you believe:

*Most assuredly, I say to you, he who hears
My word and believes in Him who sent Me
has everlasting life, and shall not come into
judgment, but has passed from death into
life. (John 5:24)*

Now let's look at the requirements Jesus gives for
being His disciple. Remember, He gives these
requirements because He loves us and wants real
intimacy with us. The things He shares with us, though
seemingly harsh, are His invitation for the greatest
intimacy with Him. Also, keep in mind the harshness of
the cross—the price He paid for intimacy with you. He
paid this price for your discipleship. In addition to this,
He wants you to consider what it will cost you to be His
disciple:

Anyone who comes to me but refuses to let go of father, mother, spouse, children, brothers, sisters—yes, even one's own self! — can't be my disciple. Anyone who won't shoulder his own cross and follow behind me can't be my disciple.

Is there anyone here who, planning to build a new house, doesn't first sit down and figure the cost so you'll know if you can complete it? If you only get the foundation laid and then run out of money, you're going to look pretty foolish. Everyone passing by will poke fun at you: "He started something he couldn't finish."

. . . Simply put, if you're not willing to take what is dearest to you, whether plans or people, and kiss it good-bye, you can't be my disciple. (Luke 14:26–33 TMSG)

I have experienced some of the cost of following Jesus as His disciple. In 1990, my wife and I were living in Indiana where we were born and raised. We, with our six children, had been a vital part of a church for about 14 years when we decided to go on a vacation to New Mexico. I will never forget the moment I stretched out on a bed in Aztec, New Mexico. I heard what I call the inward audible voice of the Lord. He said, "This is your people." I instantly knew He was speaking of the people in the Four Corners' area (the area around where Utah, Colorado, New Mexico, and Arizona meet). Then my wife and I understood why we were no longer feeling at home in Indiana but felt at home in the Four Corners' area of New Mexico.

Nine months later in the last days of June 1991, we left all of our relatives, our home, our jobs, our natural security, and followed the Lord's leading to New Mexico to preach the gospel. We had no home, no job, and no natural security. But we were being a disciple—following Jesus at whatever the cost. Even so, we were holding onto His promise in Mark 10:29–30:

> *So Jesus answered and said, "Assuredly, I say to you, there is no one who has left house or brothers or sisters or father or mother or wife or children or lands, for My sake and the gospel's, who shall not receive a hundredfold now in this time—houses and brothers and sisters and mothers and children and lands, with persecutions—and in the age to come, eternal life.*

Jesus kept His promise and blessed us with those who are like fathers, mothers, brothers, and sisters to us. In addition, we have had good jobs and have been a vital part of the local church.

I shared the above testimony so I can make the next point: I may look like His disciple to others, but what does God see? For God looks at the heart, not the outward appearance. *"For the Lord does not see as man sees; for man looks at the outward appearance, but the Lord looks at the heart"* (1 Samuel 16:7). Does God see me as His disciple?

I may have followed Jesus in the "big move" which everyone saw, but too often I have not followed Him in other things—things others do not know about. Such as, not sharing the good news with someone when the Lord leads me to, or not praying for someone's healing when I felt I should. No one but God saw my failures to follow Him. By outward appearances I may look like a disciple, but what does God see? He sees someone whose heart is loyal to Him, but not perfectly loyal. What does that mean? It means:

> *For the eyes of the Lord run to and fro throughout the whole earth, to show Himself strong on behalf of those whose heart is loyal to Him. (2 Chronicles 16:9)*

I am weak too often, but my heart is somewhat loyal to Him and He sees that and shows Himself strong on my behalf. He strengthens me to be more loyal to Him—strengthens my discipleship. Don't forget, God works in us to do what pleases Him. *"For God is working in you, giving you the desire and the power to do what pleases him"* (Philippians 2:13 NLT).

If you have not been much of a disciple, take heart because God is for you, not against you. The Scriptures show you many who were less than being the best disciple. One was even a secret disciple but came forth publicly after Jesus' death because the power for discipleship is in the cross:

> *After this, Joseph of Arimathea, being a disciple of Jesus, but secretly, for fear of the Jews, asked Pilate that he might take away*

*the body of Jesus; and Pilate gave him
permission. (John 19:38)*

The cross is the ultimate showcase of God's love and
desire for us. Seeing this love and desire for us on the
cross is the ultimate motivation for our discipleship (see
Hebrews 12:2–3).

The Scriptures also give Paul as an example of God's
power to change a person into His disciple. Paul first
persecuted the disciples, then became a great disciple
himself. Remember the words of Jesus: *"But to whom
little is forgiven, the same loves little"* (Luke 7:47).

His Commandments

Too many of us have misunderstood His
commandments. Make no mistake about it; they are
commands. That being said, we need to understand
their true purpose. *"For this is the love of God, that we
keep His commandments. And His commandments are
not burdensome"* (1 John 5:3). His commands are not
burdensome; they are actually invitations to an
unhindered relationship with Him. From His first
command, *"of the tree of the knowledge of good and
evil you shall not eat"* (Genesis 2:17), we see the
purpose of His commands—for unhindered fellowship
with Him. When Adam and Eve broke His command,
their fellowship with God was hindered. Now they knew
good and evil, lost their focus on God, focused on their
own appearance, and then tragically, they hid from God.

Is this not exactly what happens to us when we do
not keep His commandments? Is this not why we need
to see the purpose of His commands?

His commands are not for knowing good and evil, but for knowing Him unhindered—partaking of the tree of life without restriction. Truly, His commandments are an invitation to full fellowship with Him.

Jesus said, *"If you love Me, keep My commandments"* (John 14:15). We are not to keep His commandments out of duty but out of love—where you love His presence and you do not want anything hindering that love-fellowship.

Holiness is not dos and don'ts; it is responding to His invitation to live in such a way that your fellowship with God is not hindered. Simply put, holiness is an invitation to unhindered fellowship with God.

More Blessings

Being His disciple is not focusing on ourselves by constantly examining how well we are following Him. Our focus is to be on Jesus. If our focus is on Him, we will begin to feel His heart for others. Then we will realize a major purpose for our discipleship—to make disciples. This is the central part of the great commission—Jesus giving us the responsibility of making disciples.

> *"...go and make disciples of all the nations ... Teach these new disciples to obey all the commands I have given you. And be sure of this: I am with you always, even to the end of the age." (Matthew 28:19–20 NLT)*

Making disciples is a great motivation for your own discipleship. For when you see others growing in Jesus, it motivates your own growth, especially if you are the one leading them into discipleship.

A major danger in making disciples is losing the focus of discipleship—everyone following Jesus. If you do not point them to Jesus, they can easily become followers of you more than followers of the Lord. Disciples are to be in God's image, not in the image of someone else. They are fashioned to behold Him and to be *His* disciple. Of course, this does not mean that they will not be greatly influenced by you since you are their "father" or "mother" in the spiritual realm. For them, you set the example of what a disciple is to be and they will follow that to a degree.

Therefore, the greatest thing you can do for others is to set an example of love—love for God and love for others. This ability to love is the greatest image of God available to you. As His disciple, you learn to use more and more of that capacity to love. The more you love the more you are like Him. The more you model love, the more those that follow you will be like Him.

Included in our ability to love is the capacity to love grace and truth. By our example, we can teach others to love His grace and His truth. For when they see us loving these things, it motivates them to love them also. Then as they follow Jesus, they will grow in these virtues too. These virtues of grace and truth are very important for they are major parts of the foundation of our growth in Christ (we covered this in the first few chapters of this book).

Summing Up

God's best requires your best. Do not let this intimidate you because you are the temple of the Holy Spirit. Through the power of the Holy Spirit you can do anything. As Philippians 4:13 states: *"I can do all things through Christ who strengthens me."*

Though the following verse refers to material needs, it is true for everything we need. *"And my God shall supply all your need according to His riches in glory by Christ Jesus"* (Philippians 4:19).

You can follow Jesus as much as you desire because you have the power of the Holy Spirit. The Holy Spirit will teach you and bring to your remembrance the things Jesus said. The Holy Spirit is wonderful at making disciples. As you yield to Him, you are following Jesus.

A major part of following Jesus will be working in the harvest that is upon us. You will be making disciples of the new believers by teaching them to observe all things that Jesus taught. For by this time you ought to be teachers of others (see Hebrews 5:12).

The best place God has provided for discipleship is within the body of Christ. Remember, the Head of the body gave gifts to the church for helping to make disciples. If you want to be His disciple and make disciples, the best place to be is in the body of Christ.

Now What?

Precious Father, I have heard Your call, "Follow Me." You really like me and want my friendship. But I have not always responded to Your call, forgive me. For I want to follow You. I want to be Your disciple and to disciple others.

Jesus, I believe You are making me a fisherman of men and women. I pray in Your name that I catch as many as You desire—an abundant harvest. Amen.

Anyone who wants to be my disciple must follow me, because my servants must be where I am. And the Father will honor anyone who serves me.

John 12:26 NLT

Chapter 14

His Fullness

*T*he last chapter prepared us for this chapter. For His fullness actually begins with what was covered in the last chapter—discipleship. If we want to obtain His fullness, it begins with being His disciple since the motivation of a disciple is to be like his Master—to obtain His fullness. Obtaining His fullness is a growth process where we continuously grow up into Him. This process is discipleship. The end goal of discipleship is His fullness and leading others to it.

If the fullness of God is our goal, then there is no limit to how much we can obtain since God is limitless. He is the fullness of everything we need and want. Most, if not all, are searching for more joy in their life. The good news is that there is a fullness of joy available. The fullness of joy is found in God. This joy is a part of His fullness that's available to us. Again, discipleship is the pathway for this part of His fullness. As stated earlier, discipleship is about intimacy with Him—being in His presence. We are with His presence when we are following Him, which is the path of life, the very place of the fullness of joy.

> *You will show me the path of life;*
> *In Your presence is fullness of joy;*

At Your right hand are pleasures
forevermore. (Psalm 16:11)

We live in a culture that pursues joy and pleasure, but finds very little of it. As a born-again believer, you can have His fullness of joy and pleasures forevermore. Simply follow Him.

This does not mean that you will not have struggles or experience the trying of your faith; it means you can have joy in every circumstance when you are following Jesus.

> *Dear brothers and sisters, when troubles come your way, consider it an opportunity for great joy. For you know that when your faith is tested, your endurance has a chance to grow. So let it grow, for when your endurance is fully developed, you will be perfect and complete, needing nothing. (James 1:2–4 NLT)*

The reason for great joy in your testing is the fullness that is developed through the experience. When your endurance is fully developed, you enter into a fullness that would not be possible without the tests. A major test for your life will be whether you keep His commands. When you keep His commands, you keep full intimacy and the place of full joy as shown in John 15:

> *If you keep my commands, you'll remain intimately at home in my love. That's what I've done—kept my Father's commands and made myself at home in his love.*

I've told you these things for a purpose: that my joy might be your joy, and your joy wholly mature. This is my command: Love one another the way I loved you. (John 15:10–12 TMSG)

His fullness includes your friendship and the fullness of joy you have by sharing things with one another. Friends enjoy the same things, especially just being with one another. As friends, you can know that the parable in Matthew 13:44 is about the both of you:

Again, the kingdom of heaven is like treasure hidden in a field, which a man found and hid; and for joy over it he goes and sells all that he has and buys that field.

You are a treasure that God gave all He had to obtain—the death of His Son. In addition, for you, God is the hidden treasure in the field. When you find (realize) the hidden treasure God is, you will sell all (do whatever it takes) to obtain His fullness. His full friendship will be at the top of your list.

His fullness is so vast we can only cover a small portion in this chapter. We have mentioned His fullness of joy, friendship, and fully keeping His commands to maintain full intimacy. However, there is much more on God's fullness that we will not cover and God loves it when we go beyond what we cover in this book and search for Him with all our heart—as for a treasure.

Yes, He hides some things for us to find since He knows that it is part of our God-nature to be treasure hunters. The greatest treasure anyone can ever find, and have the most fun doing it, is God.

Does God really hide some things just for us to find? Yes, and it is His glory to do such a thing:

> *It is the glory of God to conceal a matter; to search out a matter is the glory of kings. (Proverbs 25:2 NIV)*

Growing in Christ is supposed to be our most fun treasure hunt. The more I have found out about Him, the more I feel I know little about Him. This causes me to search for Him more. I have found that growing in Jesus is a treasure-trove. (A treasure-trove is the place where things of great value are found.) An item of great value is either rarely found or hard to find, but that is what makes it a treasure and the find so rewarding. Growth in Christ is the best treasure we can find and the most rewarding. Even so, it may not always be the easiest treasure to find. Indeed, it may be a hard search, but when we get serious about finding all of Him, we will.

> *When you come looking for me, you'll find me.*
>
> *Yes, when you get serious about finding me and want it more than anything else, I'll make sure you won't be disappointed. God's Decree. (Jeremiah 29:13–14 TMSG)*

We will now look at the fundamental nature of the treasure of His fullness.

His Essence

As stated, His fullness requires discipleship. You cannot obtain His fullness without first being His disciple. And just like discipleship, His fullness requires a comprehension of His love. This comprehension is not just head knowledge; it is an understanding of the heart. This understanding of His love comes by the power of the Holy Spirit. By the Spirit, we understand that God is not just full of love; He *is* love—it is His very essence. Only through His Spirit can we fully comprehend this love. Then after an understanding of His love, we have the opportunity to be filled with all His fullness.

> *That He would grant you, according to the riches of His glory, to be strengthened with might through His Spirit in the inner man, that Christ may dwell in your hearts through faith; that you, being rooted and grounded in love, may be able to comprehend with all the saints what is the width and length and depth and height—to know the love of Christ which passes knowledge; that you may be filled with all the fullness of God. (Ephesians 3:16–19)*

God's essence is love. By understanding His love, we can be filled with Him. Our ultimate pursuit is God and His love. The Scripture commands us to pursue love (see 1 Corinthians 14:1). If our ultimate pursuit is love, then we will be pursuing God since God is love.

Yes, our greatest purpose is to pursue loving God and others more. Jesus even prayed that the Father's love, the same love He has for His Son, would be in us (see John 17). If we ever love like that, it will be our greatest achievement and our greatest growth.

There is no greater fullness than His love—His essence. In fact, we see that all of creation is waiting for the revelation of the sons of God who have entered into His fullness—the ones that have learned to love God and others. These ones will do whatever it takes to win God's battle. God's battle is with anything not of love— personified in the devil and his followers. But the sons of God will overcome all evil by their love of God (see Romans 8:19–22).

This seems to be the reason why the devil's main tactic is to cause our love to grow cold. For it is the good news of the gospel (the love of God) that will defeat him. Jesus had this to say about the end of this age:

> *And because lawlessness will abound, the love of many will grow cold. But he who endures to the end shall be saved. And this gospel of the kingdom will be preached in all the world as a witness to all the nations, and then the end will come. (Matthew 24:12–14)*

Because the love of God defeats the devil, there is a war against those desiring to obtain the fullness of God. For the fullness of God (love) defeats the fullness of the devil (hate).

The Change

To experience His fullness requires change. I had a dream while writing this book that explains this in picture form.

The Dream:

I was on a bed with several coins. I needed to count out one hundred dollars in coins. Trying to count the correct amount of coins on the bed was challenging. As long as I kept the coins on the bed, I made progress in counting the necessary amount of coins. But if I got to close to the edge, the coins would fall to the floor and I would have to start over, although just with the coins that fell.

The Interpretation:

The coins speak of "change" since coins are often referred to as change. The amount of change needed, one hundred dollars, speaks of the necessary change I need—a lot of change. However, all of the change I need is available on the bed. The bed speaks of intimacy. The correct change I need comes from intimacy—the bed/God's presence—the place of rest. Getting the change I need is challenging but can easily be accomplished if I stay on the bed—His rest, intimacy. If I get too close to the edge of the bed I may lose my balance and the change may fall by the wayside. Then I need to re-count (remember) the change that was lost over the side of the bed. I then could retrieve that change, place it on the bed (intimacy), and add that change back into what I need.

The point of the dream in a few words: He invites you to the place of intimacy where you can "count on" the Lord for the "change" you need. Certainly, the main point of the dream is that change comes through intimacy with God—resting with Him in His finished work—spending time with Him. You can do this by praying, reading His word, meditating on Him, praising Him, thanking Him, soaking in His presence, or however the Lord leads you to be with Him. Then do the things He directs you to do.

When I was the pastor of a church, I often wondered what Jesus would say to the church. Would He speak to the church as I am? How would He encourage the church? After all, He is the Shepherd of the sheep (see John 10:11).

The answer I believe I was given is Hebrews 13:8: *"Jesus Christ is the same yesterday, today, and forever."* This led me to when Jesus spoke to the seven churches in Revelation chapters 2 and 3. The following is a quote from a previous book I wrote:

> How did He speak to the churches in the past? Revelation chapters 2 and 3 give us the answer. These two chapters reveal the heart of Jesus as He speaks to His church. He loves His church so much that He speaks to her with full grace and truth. In these chapters, Jesus speaks to the seven churches of the first century. Many believe the seven literal churches spoken of in Asia also represent seven eras of church history with the Laodicean church being the church at the end of the age. Even so, you do not want to overlook Jesus' messages to all of the churches because He has a message for every type of church. He has a message for any church that:
>
> 1) Left its first love.
>
> 2) Is persecuted and poor.

3) Is a compromising, worldly church.

4) Is an immoral church.

5) Is lifeless.

6) Is faithful.

7) Is lukewarm.

I believe the church that most represents our day is the Laodicean church—the lukewarm church. Why would Jesus call the church of our day lukewarm? *"Because you say, 'I am rich, have become wealthy, and have need of nothing'—and do not know that you are wretched, miserable, poor, blind, and naked . . ."* (Revelation 3:17).

Jesus speaks the truth to us without compromise. He wants us to know our condition so we change course. Lukewarmness blinds our eyes and unless Jesus by His grace tells us the truth, we will never change.

So how can we change? Jesus tells us: *"I counsel you to buy from Me gold refined in the fire, that you may be rich; and white garments, that you may be clothed, that the shame of your nakedness may not be revealed; and anoint your eyes with eye salve, that you may see"* (Revelation 3:18).

Lukewarmness is hard to overcome because we think that we are okay; we feel we have everything we need. We do not know how poor we are until Jesus speaks the truth to us. When we know the truth that is what sets us free.

Jesus speaks the truth to us in love. He said, *"As many as I love, I rebuke and chasten. Therefore be zealous and repent"* (Revelation 3:19).

—*Steven J. Campbell*
Well Done: Good and Faithful Servant,
pgs. 101–102.

In Revelation chapters 2 and 3, Jesus ends His address to each church with: *"He who has an ear, let him hear what the Spirit says to the churches."* By saying this, He validates His message to all of the seven churches as being for everyone who has an ear—let him hear.

In those two chapters, Jesus is inviting us to overcome everything that is hindering our walk with Him. He is not just telling us what is right and wrong with us. He is inviting us to a fullness of fellowship with Him. Notice also that we are to *"hear what the Spirit says to the churches."* This indicates a level of intimacy to be able to hear the Spirit and understand what He is saying. Real change comes through His word and intimacy—hearing the Spirit.

His fullness involves relationship with the Holy Spirit. Without a relationship with the Holy Spirit His fullness seems to be unattainable since the Spirit is the One who leads us to Jesus. Furthermore, God's method to obtain His fullness is by the Spirit working through His body—the church. Again, a relationship to His church is vital for our growth into His fullness. We see this stated in Ephesians 4:11–13:

> *And He Himself gave some to be apostles, some prophets, some evangelists, and some pastors and teachers, for the equipping of the saints for the work of ministry, for the edifying of the body of Christ, till we all come to the unity of the faith and of the knowledge of the Son of God, to a perfect man, to the measure of the stature of the fullness of Christ.*

We can obtain His fullness—*"the stature of the fullness of Christ"*—because He gives us all the grace we need. *"But to each one of us grace was given according to the measure of Christ's gift"* (Ephesians 4:7). And out of His fullness we have all received the necessary grace.

> *And of His fullness we have all received, and grace for grace. For the law was given through Moses, but grace and truth came through Jesus Christ. (John 1:16–17)*

We will end this chapter, having only touched on some of the issues of His fullness, with Hebrews 11:6:

> *But without faith it is impossible to please Him, for he who comes to God must believe that He is, and that He is a rewarder of those who diligently seek Him.*

Always believe that God rewards the seekers of Him, but apply this verse personally—that God will reward your seeking of Him. Yes, He will reward you with His fullness if you diligently seek Him in harmony with the Scriptures.

Now What?

Father, I believe I can have more of Your fullness as I follow the Holy Spirit. Help me to listen to Your Holy Spirit so that I may hear His voice and follow Him.

Holy Spirit, stir my hunger for more of You.

Jesus, You are offering Your fullness to me; will You fan the ember of hunger in my heart for You into a roaring flame? I want You to. I don't want to be lukewarm. I want to be hot for You. Let Your eyes that are like a flame of fire ignite my heart. In Your name I pray. Amen.

Oh, my dear children! I feel as if I'm going through labor pains for you again, and they will continue until Christ is fully developed in your lives.

Galatians 4:19 NLT

Chapter 15

Lovesick

by Austin J. Campbell

From my earliest days I remember knowing who God is. I gave my life to Jesus at five-years-old. There wasn't much that I heard in Sunday School or Youth Group that I didn't know already thanks to my wonderful parents, who filled my head and heart daily with the things of God.

I now know that this isn't true for everybody, but in my younger years, I thought everybody in church was raised as I was, with the Bible for breakfast, lunch and dinner.

I discovered the sad truth over time. When I would talk to other kids my age about the things of God, their response was either confusion or the expression of "I'm hearing this for the first time." That was my first memory of godly heartbreak. Realizing that most kids my age knew little about God was devastating.

I tell this part of the story to give you an idea of my reputation. I was a good pastor's kid who knew and loved God more than all the other kids. The problem: it was merely that—a reputation. I was like the Church of Sardis in the Book of Revelation: *"...I know your works, that you have a name that you are alive, but you are dead"* (3:1).

I may have impressed people with my displays of knowledge and riding on my parents' true spiritual relationship, but God wasn't impressed.

I became increasingly restless on the inside when I reached my teen years. I needed to become "my own person," and I was, but not on the inside. As everything else about me was becoming an adult, my spiritual life was still in kindergarten.

In the summer of 2006, at the age of sixteen, I decided to do something about it. I started to read the Bible for myself. Nothing profound seemed to happen when I read it, but I kept reading anyway. One day a close friend of mine, Rebekah, opened up Matthew 24 to me. She explained things about that chapter I had never heard before. She was teaching me about the end-times, and my heart came alive. This was the jump-start I needed.

I decided to start going to church with her, along with my younger sister and brother. We would go to our church's little, dark prayer room and just wait on God. A most miraculous thing happened, God's presence showed up. Sometimes we would cry. Sometimes we would laugh. Whatever happened didn't matter to us, we just wanted God.

We did this on a consistent basis for about three months, going to the prayer room to "meet with God." It was wonderful. The Holy Spirit would reveal how Jesus thinks and feels about me, and often I would be moved to tears. Instead of only a knowledge of God, I had encountered Him. It was as if I had heard about this Person for years and I was finally meeting Him for the first time. I felt like the Shulamite in the Song of Solomon:

> *Like an apple tree among the trees of the woods, so is my beloved among the sons. I sat down in his shade with great delight, and his fruit was sweet to my taste. (2:3)*

It was a time of refreshing, when it wasn't about me doing anything, I was just suppose to enjoy Jesus.

After the three months, for whatever reason, the feeling of Jesus' nearness began to wane. There were enough fumes from the spiritual high to keep me going for another three months, but then I fell flat on my face. I needed Jesus in a real and tangible way, but He was nowhere to be found.

"I Am Lovesick"

"I charge you . . . if you find my beloved, that you tell him I am lovesick!" (Song of Solomon 5:8).

Let us define what it is to be lovesick: it is the ache between desire and fulfillment. If you love someone but all your longings for them are fulfilled immediately, you could never use the phrase "I was lovesick for them," because you never gave the desire enough time to grow. When fulfillment is delayed, the desire will either grow or fade, it is never static. In a time of longing, offense may settle in our heart, causing us to lose interest in the relationship, but if we choose to keep seeking, desire may become a raging fire on the inside. The NIV translation calls this *"faint with love."* This kind of love is not a trivial thing we can ignore.

When we first come to Christ, love is in the air! It seems every other breath is spent telling people about His mercy and compassion. However, a hundred times out of a hundred, I see this happen to new believers: the feeling wanes.

Whether it is the failure of the believer to guard against disappointment and sin, or if it is a God-ordained test, the result is the same—God feels far away. At this moment, it is an opportunity for one of the greatest spiritual gifts on this side of eternity. We can choose to either dull this pain with the inferior pleasures of sin, or let the ache grow. If lovesickness grows, it can lead us to the greatest pleasures in God we've ever known.

As stated earlier, being lovesick is like having a fire in the heart. The heat cannot be ignored. If we hate the feeling, we try to put it out with other inferior things we enjoy. If we love the flame, we stoke the fire and make it hotter—if we feel dull, we fast; if we feel alone, we pray; if we don't feel His love, we give it away; if we have a moral failing; we repent and pursue holiness. This is how we stoke the fire.

Let us return to the Song of Solomon to see what happened to the Shulamite in this situation.

> *I sleep, but my heart is awake;*
> *It is the voice of my beloved!*
> *He knocks, saying,*
> *"Open for me, my sister, my love,*

My dove, my perfect one". . .

*My beloved put his hand by the latch of
     the door,
And my heart yearned for him.
I arose to open for my beloved . . .
But my beloved had turned away and
     was gone.
My heart leaped up when he spoke.
I sought him, but I could not find him;
I called him, but he gave me no answer.
     (Song of Solomon 5:2–6)*

We see that the Shulamite is feeling genuine love for her beloved. She moves toward him and seeks after him, but to no avail. He is gone.

Instead of being offended, she continues to seek. Throughout all the Shulamite's interactions, the "Daughters of Jerusalem" are observing from a distance. In a spiritual context, I liken the Daughters of Jerusalem to fellow believers in Christ. We are commanded to surround ourselves with brothers and sisters in the faith, for our own good (Hebrews 10:24–25). Many times it is in the context of church life that we feel fulfilled and encouraged in Christ, yet, sadly, many times it is the same place we are hurt the most.

I am grateful that we are given the negative example in verse 7 of the Song of Solomon: *"The watchmen who went about the city found me. They struck me, they wounded me; the keepers of the walls took my veil away from me."*

Two things become clear in this verse. 1) The leaders hurt her. 2) It was mostly by their misunderstanding her.

A most remarkable thing happens in the next verse:

> *I charge you, O daughters of Jerusalem, if you find my beloved, that you tell him I am lovesick! (Song of Solomon 5:8)*

Instead of offense, she displays humility and submission to her leaders, yearning to learn whatever she can from them. She knows it is in the context of the church body that she will find him again. This is what a true disciple of Christ looks like.

We must guard against personal offense. This wound is the main cause of losing tenderness with God and people. When offended, we isolate ourselves and become bitter. It is inevitable that we will be mistreated in this life, but the decision to be offended is not.

My Own Offense

In July of 2014, my friend Rebekah, my oldest brother Aaron and I went to a Christian conference in Colorado Springs called Desperation. At the first session, during the worship time, I noticed I was having difficulty connecting my heart with Jesus. I thought I had dealt with most of the bitterness that accumulated through my 24 years on the earth, but a wrong assumption it was.

I wanted to find out what the issue was, so I asked the Holy Spirit, "What's going on?" Instantly, in my mind's eye, something like a scene from a movie played before me. I had never seen the characters or the place before, but that wasn't important, I needed to hear what they had to say.

There was a man about sixty-years-old sitting inside an old and weathered truck. On the passenger's seat beside him was a seven-year-old who I assumed to be his grandson. With a serious look in his eyes, the child asked his grandfather, "How are you so happy all the time?"

The old man matched the boy's serious tone, "No matter what happens in life, don't be angry. Don't get offended."

Immediately I knew he meant a festering anger and offense that leads to bitterness. As the scene before my eyes faded, a feeling of anger began to rise up in my heart. It was my own bitterness toward God, which was a surprise to me, since in the two years before I had been intentionally forgiving those who had wronged me in the past. Even so, I was fighting against bitterness in my soul, even toward God—how was it still there?

Then I heard in my heart what the anger was. It was the residual anger from the time in 2006 when God felt distant. Instead of properly discerning God's "distance" as a test to push deeper into our relationship, I saw it as His neglect.

As soon as it was clear exactly what the anger was, I gave it up. I signed up again to go after an open heart toward God and people. I wanted to be like the old man in the old truck—happy.

"He is My Beloved"

The Holy Spirit is the Comforter, and He will heal all our brokenness. With His help, we can go through trials. Let us learn from the Shulamite and forgive those that do us wrong.

Because of her humility back in Song of Solomon 5:8, and her refusal to become offended and draw back from seeking after her beloved, it opened a door to clear up the misunderstanding from before. *"What is your beloved more than another beloved . . . ?"* (5:9), the Daughters of Jerusalem ask.

Now they are seeking her counsel. It would be like an older, much wiser person in the church coming up to you and saying, "What do you know about God that I don't?" This is a marvelous statement.

Then she spends the next seven verses (10–16) describing the beauty of Jesus, why He is worth the misunderstanding, the ache, the lovesickness.

> *He alone is my Beloved.*
> *He shines in dazzling splendor,*
> *Yet still so approachable.*
> *Without equal as He stands above all others*
> *   —waving His banner to myriads!*
> *The way He leads me is divine.*
> *His leadership—so pure and dignified as He*
> *   wears His crown of gold.*
> *Upon this crown are letters of black written*
> *   on a background of glory.*
> *He sees everything with pure understanding.*

How beautiful His insights—without
*   distortion.*
His eyes rest upon the fullness of the river of
*   revelation flowing so clean and pure!*
Looking at His gentle face I see such fullness
*   of emotion.*
Like a lovely garden where fragrant spices
*   grow—what a Man!*
No one speaks words so anointed as this
*   One—words that both pierce and heal,*
Words like lilies dripping with myrrh.
See how His hands hold unlimited power!
But He never uses it in anger,
For He is always holy, displaying His glory.
His innermost place is a work of art—
So beautiful and bright.
How magnificent and noble is this One—
Covered in majesty!
He's steadfast in all He does,
Never veering.
His ways are the ways of righteousness,
Based on truth and holiness.
None can rival Him,
But all will be amazed by Him!
Most sweet are His kisses,
Even His whispers of love.
He is delightful in every way and perfect
*   from every viewpoint.*
If you ask me why I love Him so,
O brides-to-be,
It is because there is none like Him to me.

> *Everything about Him fills me with holy*
> *desire!*
> *And now He is my Beloved—my forever*
> *Friend! (Song of Songs 5:10–16 TPT)*

What happens when she displays so much humility, and then goes on and on about the beauty of Jesus? The Daughters of Jerusalem are provoked to pursue this holy love with her.

> *"Where has your beloved gone . . . that we*
> *may seek him with you?"*
> *(Song of Solomon 6:1)*

It was the test of staying humble, teachable and tender toward Jesus that she passed with flying colors because of His beauty that was before her eyes, not the trouble, but the reward. Then the silence is broken. Her Beloved cannot contain Himself.

> *"O my love, you are as beautiful as Tirzah,*
> *Lovely as Jerusalem,*
> *Awesome as an army with banners!"*
> *(Song of Solomon 6:4)*

Her beauty is described as being "an army with banners," as in, "she is victorious in battle." Not only has she "conquered" Jesus' heart in love, but also she was victorious over her greatest enemy, her own soul. Nothing stood in her way when it came to love; no offense, no trial, no slander, no waiting, and not even sin. His love was the reward.

The Spirit and the Bride

To clarify, Jesus is not far from us, but there are secrets that are deeper than we understand right now. God knows that the more effort we exert to know His secrets, the more it will affect us in the deep parts of the soul.

I don't believe lovesickness will ever completely go away on this side of eternity. Once it begins in your life, it should continue on, not in the way that you always feel God is far off (that should be a rare thing), but in the way that there's an itch in your soul that says, "There's got to be more!" I believe it is God's plan to keep us in the ache of longing, because the ache drives us to holiness, to prayer, to communion with the Holy Spirit and fellowship with other believers.

At the end of the story, it is the Holy Spirit and the people of God, affectionately called the Bride, crying out with deep longing for Jesus, *"Come!"* (see Revelation 22:17).

My soul thirsts for God, for the living God.

When can I go and meet with God?

Psalm 42:2 NIV

Chapter 16

Homesick

*A*s born again believers, we ought to be homesick. But what does that mean? We are using the word *homesick* to mean: a yearning, a hunger, a craving, a thirsting for home. So where is our home that we are longing for? We will look at the obvious and the less obvious answers.

First, we want to see why we would be homesick. We are homesick because we are lovesick. To the extent that we are lovesick, we are homesick. Our son Austin did a fantastic job of writing the last chapter, *Lovesick*. The last chapter is directly connected to this chapter.

We should never be ashamed to confess our lovesickness for Jesus before others or before Him.

> *I charge you, O daughters of Jerusalem,*
> *If you find my beloved,*
> *That you tell him I am lovesick!*
> *(Song of Solomon 5:8)*

Love is contagious. And there is nothing more contagious than God's love. God wants us fully contagious—lovesick *and* homesick. How do we become lovesick and homesick? We become lovesick and then homesick by being in His presence. Being in His presence is being in His love, which is contagious. *"We love Him because He first loved us"* (1 John 4:19). His passion of love for us ignites our passion of love for Him.

His love caused our love; so likewise, our homesickness will cause others to be homesick. The question is: "Do you really want to be homesick and cause others to be homesick?" As you understand what homesickness is, I think your answer will be, "Yes!"

I am dividing this chapter into four parts: *Homesick for Heaven, Homesick for Heaven on Earth, Homesick for the Commander,* and *Homesick for the City.*

Homesick for Heaven

The most obvious homesickness is the longing for heaven—being face to face with God. We find our home in God because He first found His home in us—we are a temple of the Holy Spirit. God is our home and we yearn to be with Him. The face-to-face companionship with God is what we were created for (see Genesis 3:8–9). This type of face-to-face friendship brings a fullness of joy just as 2 John 12 shows:

> *Having many things to write to you, I did not wish to do so with paper and ink; but I hope to come to you and speak face to face, that our joy may be full.*

Actually, we are already with God. He lives in us! Nevertheless there is much more we will know and experience when we are in heaven—we can know God now, but not in the fullness of being with Him face to face.

*Now we see but a poor reflection as in a
mirror; then we shall see face to face. Now I
know in part; then I shall know fully, even as
I am fully known. (1 Corinthians 13:12 NIV)*

Because Paul knew this, he was homesick to be with
the Lord—his true home:

*So we are always confident, even though we
know that as long as we live in these bodies
we are not at home with the Lord. For we
live by believing and not by seeing. Yes, we
are fully confident, and we would rather be
away from these earthly bodies, for then we
will be at home with the Lord. (2 Corinthians
5:6–9 NLT)*

I want to go to heaven to be with God face to face, but
like Paul and Jesus, I want my time on earth to be
accomplished first. Jesus finished His work, and then
died (see John 19:30). Paul also knew he must finish his
work of service before going to heaven. However, it is
not an easy choice to make when you are homesick:

*For to me, living means living for Christ, and
dying is even better. But if I live, I can do
more fruitful work for Christ. So I really
don't know which is better. I'm torn between
two desires: I long to go and be with Christ,
which would be far better for me. But for
your sakes, it is better that I continue to live.*

*Knowing this, I am convinced that I will
remain alive so I can continue to help all of*

you grow and experience the joy of your faith. (Philippians 1:21–25 NLT)

I too must be unselfish—wait to go home until my work is finished.

You may be homesick to meet Jesus—but He is more excited to meet you face to face. You want to meet the Father personally, but Jesus wants you to meet His Father more than you do. For sure, He will personally introduce you to the Father! This is the highlight of going to heaven—being reunited with the Father face to face. Jesus might even dance for joy over you as He introduces you! Thinking about this might make you homesick.

But never forget you are already one with Him, even though your ultimate destination is His face-to-face presence. So don't just wait for His face-to-face presence when you can have so much of his presence now. Draw close to God and He will draw close to you (see James 4:8).

The more you enjoy God, the more you want to be with Him. The more you want to be with Him, the more homesick you become. *"I'm homesick, God, for your salvation; I love it when you show yourself!"* (Psalm 119:174 TMSG).

Another thing that can make us homesick for heaven is the promises Jesus gives us—to those that hear His invitation to overcome and actually overcome (see Revelation 2–3):

1. To eat from the tree of life in the midst of the Paradise of God.

2. To give us the crown of life.

3. To give us some of the hidden manna to eat and a white stone with a new name written which no one knows except him who receives it.

4. To give us the morning star.

5. To confess our name before the Father and the angels.

6. To make us a pillar in the temple of God and have the name of God, the name of the city of God, and Jesus' new name written on us.

7. To sit with Jesus on His throne.

There is a danger of homesickness for heaven. That danger could be called "spiritual suicide"—going home before our work is finished—or even wanting to go home so much that we ignore the present. Our present home, and not just our future home, is to be a part of our homesickness as the next section will show us.

Homesick for Heaven on Earth

Did you know that our real home is not some far off place called heaven? Our real home is God and where He is. Heaven is wherever God is. When we use the phrase when someone dies as his or her "going home," this is many times misinterpreted. It is misinterpreted in the sense that leaving earth gets you to your real home. However, this is not entirely accurate. Yes, it is accurate in the sense that God, and where He is, is our true home. But it is not accurate in the physical sense.

Our home is the earth, for God created humans to inhabit this planet.

When we "go home" to be with the Lord (heaven) we are in a sense leaving our home. Why? Because our time in heaven (the place beyond earth where God is) is only temporary. God's realm (heaven) is actually coming to earth. In fact, we are all coming back home (to earth) when Jesus comes back.

> *And now, dear brothers and sisters, we want you to know what will happen to the believers who have died so you will not grieve like people who have no hope. For since we believe that Jesus died and was raised to life again, we also believe that when Jesus returns, God will bring back with him the believers who have died.*
> *(1 Thessalonians 4:13–14 NLT)*

Notice that it says God will *bring back* with Him all the believers. We are coming back to earth. This will be the time when we all will receive our new incorruptible bodies and meet the Lord in the clouds—*of the earth* (see 1 Thessalonians 4:15–18).

Too many of us have committed "spiritual suicide" with our overemphasis on the rapture—focusing on getting out of this world—leaving the earth—instead of fulfilling our purpose on the earth. Too many have forgotten Jesus' mission was not to condemn the world but to save it. He saved the world in multiple ways:

> *The Spirit of the Lord is upon Me,*
> *Because He has anointed Me*

To preach the gospel to the poor;
He has sent Me to heal the brokenhearted,
To proclaim liberty to the captives
And recovery of sight to the blind,
To set at liberty those who are oppressed;
To proclaim the acceptable year of the Lord.
(Luke 4:18–19)

And Jesus gives us the same mission: *"As the Father has sent Me, I also send you"* (John 20:21).

Yes, God is making a new earth for us to live in but He also made us for living on the earth now. He wants us to pray for His will to be done on earth as it is in heaven. And as I wrote in my last book, *Well Done: Good and Faithful Servant*, He expects us to use the talents He gives us to bring heaven to earth according to the measure of our giftings. Our giftings given us by the Spirit of the Lord will result in us fulfilling one or more of the Lord's salvations spoken of in Luke 4:18–19 above.

As we truly begin to pray—*"Our Father in heaven, hallowed be Your name. Your kingdom come. Your will be done on earth as it is in heaven. Give us day by day our daily bread. And forgive us our sins, for we also forgive everyone who is indebted to us. And do not lead us into temptation, but deliver us from the evil one"* (Luke 11:2–4)—we will be homesick for heaven on earth and not just concerned about leaving here as soon as possible.

Our mission is not just to get to heaven as soon as possible, but to leave as much of heaven on earth as possible through living our lives here. We are to leave a deposit of heaven on earth before we die. If we are homesick for heaven on earth, we will not cut our "deposit of heaven" here short. The more homesick for heaven on earth we are the greater deposit of heaven we will leave.

Love is the greatest deposit of heaven that we can leave here. Actually, we are to have and leave here the very same contagious love that the Father has. He is lovesick for His Son. He is lovesick for you. He is homesick for you to be where He is (see John 17:24). Nonetheless, He put you on earth for you to learn to *enjoy* Him **here** and to transmit to others that same enjoyment of God. We are to be that lovesick—to have a contagious enjoyment of God. The more we enjoy God the more of the homesickness for heaven on earth we release.

According to Acts 3:21, Jesus will stay in heaven *until* the times of the restoration of all things. One of the things God promises to restore is the tabernacle of David. David enjoyed God. He released the enjoyment of God on earth, especially through song. He did this by realizing how much God enjoyed him, and as a result, opened the eyes of countless others to the fact that God enjoys us. Yes, He enjoys weak, imperfect people, like David; in fact, He gave us David as an example of this so that we may know God enjoys us, and that we can all enjoy God.

When Jesus came, He said that the kingdom of heaven is at hand. He made heaven real on earth, so much so, that His followers were sorrowful when He told them He was leaving earth. They thought that the heaven on earth Jesus released would be lessened, but that is not what Jesus believed. He said:

> ... *I tell you the truth. It is to your advantage that I go away; for if I do not go away, the Helper will not come to you; but if I depart, I will send Him to you. (John 16:7)*

Jesus knew that the heaven on earth would increase when the Holy Spirit came, not decrease. Furthermore, He said that heaven on earth (the kingdom at hand) is to be our message and our demonstration.

> *And as you go, preach, saying, "The kingdom of heaven is at hand." Heal the sick, cleanse the lepers, raise the dead, cast out demons. Freely you have received, freely give. (Matthew 10:7–8)*

Jesus believed that there would *not* be a reduction of heaven on earth because He left. He emphatically states this truth in John 14:12:

> *Most assuredly, I say to you, he who believes in Me, the works that I do he will do also; and greater works than these he will do, because I go to My Father.*

A final key to bringing heaven to earth is the Scriptures themselves. *All* Scripture is the very breath of God (God-breathed) as 2 Timothy 3:16 states. Therefore, the Scriptures themselves are a part of the heaven on earth we are homesick for. Because of this, we may not be taken seriously about being homesick for heaven on earth if we ignore the reading and studying of the Bible.

A major part of heaven on earth is the stories, teachings, and prophecies of the Bible. The Bible brings heaven to earth by releasing memories of the past, present, and future. That is, we know heaven's perspective of past events, present situations, and even future events because of the Bible. It's true; I have memories of the future (things that have not happened yet) because of the Bible. An example of this is that I know and remember that I will have a new glorified body and will forever be with the Lord because the Bible tells me so—even though it has not happened yet. Yes, the memories given by God are eternal.

In conclusion to this section, we want to point out the major purpose for our being homesick for heaven on earth. We are homesick for building God a home on earth—He wants to inhabit (abide) in people on the earth.

The Spirit of Christ is to leave heaven and serve on the earth. When we are more concerned about finishing our ministry on earth than going to heaven, we are imitating Christ. He was more concerned about others than Himself. He *left* heaven because He was very concerned about making the love of God obvious to all. He embraced the cross (the finishing of His ministry on earth) to show how much the Father loves us—even those that crucified Him. *"Then Jesus said, 'Father, forgive them, for they do not know what they do'"* (Luke 23:34).

Homesick for the Commander

At first, it may seem odd to be homesick for a commander. However, as the days we live in become more and more intense, we will begin to experience this type of homesickness. So what exactly is this homesickness? Like all homesickness, it is rooted in our true home—God. It is the homesickness for a specific aspect of God, which is one of the names of God—in the Hebrew language, ADONAI TZVA'OT—the LORD of Hosts. To introduce this subject I want to look at the experience Joshua had right before the battle at Jericho.

> *Now when Joshua was near Jericho, he looked up and saw a man standing in front of him with a drawn sword in his hand. Joshua went up to him and asked, "Are you for us or for our enemies?"*
>
> *"Neither," he replied, "but as commander of the army of the LORD I have now come." Then Joshua fell facedown to the ground in reverence, and asked him, "What message does my Lord have for his servant?"*
>
> *The commander of the LORD's army replied, "Take off your sandals, for the place where you are standing is holy." And Joshua did so. (Joshua 5:13–15 NIV)*

I believe the Lord has the same message for us as He did for Joshua—*"the place where you are standing is holy."* We are standing in just such holy days. In these holy days, the issue is not whether He is for us or for our adversaries, but the issue is His holiness. Too many of us have separated God's warrior nature from His holiness. However, His warrior nature is a *major* part of His holiness and a central part of His glory as Psalm 24 states:

> *Who is the King of glory?*
> *The Lord, strong and mighty; the Lord,*
>   *invincible in battle.*
> *Open up, ancient gates!*
> *Open up, ancient doors, and let the King of*
>   *glory enter.*
> *Who is the King of glory?*
> *The Lord of Heaven's Armies—he is the King*
>   *of glory.*
>   *(Psalm 24:8–10 NLT)*

As every day passes, we need the Commander more since the world is changing so fast—lawlessness is increasing rapidly. Because of this, we need His leadership more than ever. Yet, many of us have almost apologized for God being a warrior, mighty in battle. Why? Because we have not understood this aspect of His holiness. For sure, God is love. Thus, whatever God does is love even if we do not see it that way. Even so, our ideas about His love will change as the Commander reveals Himself in these days.

We need to open up the ancient gates, the ancient doors, and let the King of glory enter as Psalm 24 proclaims. Then He will reveal His holiness and love, which may not be understood at first. However, He does promise us *clear* understanding in the days to come.

*This is what the Lord of Heaven's Armies
says to his people:*

*". . . Look! The Lord's anger bursts out like a
storm, a whirlwind that swirls down on the
heads of the wicked. The anger of the Lord
will not diminish until it has finished all he
has planned. In the days to come you will
understand all this very clearly." (Jeremiah
23:16, 19–20 NLT)*

Jesus is coming back as King (the Commander). The
end-time harvesters will want and need both the King
and His kingdom. Without the Commander of heaven's
army, there will not be His great end-time harvest and
His kingdom on earth.

Having said all of this, keep in mind that God is not
angry with you, His child, because Jesus bore God's
anger for your sin on the cross. You have been saved
from the wrath of God.

*So through Christ we will surely be saved
from God's anger, because we have been
made right with God by the blood of Christ's
death. While we were God's enemies, he
made us his friends through the death of his
Son. Surely, now that we are his friends, he
will save us through his Son's life. (Romans
5:9–10 NCV)*

Even with the wicked—*"those who stubbornly follow
their own desires"* (Jeremiah 23:17 NLT)—God is slow to
anger, *"not willing that any should perish but that all
should come to repentance"* (see 2 Peter 3:9). Even so,

in the book of the revelation of Jesus Christ (Revelation 1:1) we see those that refuse to follow Him hiding from His wrath. His wrath is a very serious and *holy* thing.

> *And the kings of the earth, the great men, the rich men, the commanders, the mighty men, every slave and every free man, hid themselves in the caves and in the rocks of the mountains, and said to the mountains and rocks, "Fall on us and hide us from the face of Him who sits on the throne and from the wrath of the Lamb! For the great day of His wrath has come, and who is able to stand?" (Revelation 6:15–17)*

So why should we be homesick for such a warrior God? Because, as we stated, it is a major part of His holiness and His glory. In fact, I counted almost three hundred times that the phrase *Lord of hosts* is used in the Bible. Which means, He is referred to as the Commander of heaven's army as much, or more, than all His other titles.

The Scriptures show several other reasons why we would be homesick for our Commander to finish His work on the earth. We will look at a few of them.

First, as Commander, He deals with the pride of humankind and removes all of the gods of the earth, which results in people worshipping God:

> *This is what they get for their bloated pride, their taunts and mockeries of the people of God-of-the-Angel-Armies.*

God will be seen as truly terrible—a Holy Terror. All earth-made gods will shrivel up and blow away; and everyone, wherever they are, far or near, will fall to the ground and worship him. (Zephaniah 2:10–11 TMSG)

We will worship Him because when He comes as the Commander we will see it as His merciful love—because if He did not come, we would destroy the earth and ourselves, which is another reason to be homesick for Him.

Yet another reason to be homesick for the Commander is that when He comes He will restore everything as good as new.

But the time is coming when you're going to hear laughter and celebration, marriage festivities, people exclaiming, "Thank God-of-the-Angel-Armies. He's so good! His love never quits," as they bring thank offerings into God's Temple. I'll restore everything that was lost in this land. I'll make everything as good as new. I, God, say so. (Jeremiah 33:11 TMSG)

But before the Commander restores everything, He will shake everything that can be shaken—a very good thing because this will bring many people to Jesus—a further reason to be homesick for the Commander.

For thus says the Lord of hosts: "Once more (it is a little while) I will shake heaven and earth, the sea and dry land; and I will shake

The greatest treasures that will come to the Lord of
hosts are the people of the nations. He is the *"Desire of
All Nations."* Nevertheless, it will take the shaking of the
nations for the people to come to Him. And we are living
in such a time—the great shaking of nations. Recently, I
heard what I call an "inward audible voice." This is when
the Lord speaks so clearly to you it is as if you heard it
with your ears. He said to, "Shuttle what I shake." I
believe what He is saying to us is: Bring to Me the things
you see Me shaking on earth. In other words, intercede
(pray) for those being shaken that they would come to
know the Desire of All Nations—Jesus. For we are living
in the time of the greatest harvest of souls ever.

As you read this, it would be an excellent time to
pray for anyone that the Lord puts on your heart, or
even nations of people who are being shaken. You can
use the following Scripture to remind God of His
promise to bring many people to Himself:

*Many nations will join themselves to the
Lord on that day, and they, too, will be my
people. I will live among you, and you will
know that the Lord of Heaven's Armies sent
me to you. (Zechariah 2:11 NLT)*

You are a part of God's army. As you pray, you are
using one of the most powerful weapons available to
you. If you want to use the *most* powerful weapon you

have, combine your love for someone with prayer. By doing this, you send supernatural power into their life.

> *We are human, but we don't wage war as humans do. We use God's mighty weapons, not worldly weapons, to knock down the strongholds of human reasoning and to destroy false arguments. We destroy every proud obstacle that keeps people from knowing God. We capture their rebellious thoughts and teach them to obey Christ. (2 Corinthians 10:3–5 NLT)*

He is making us into mighty warriors to fight His end-time battles. We are mighty warriors because of the mighty warrior inside of us (the Commander—Jesus). And this mighty power is released through us as we depend upon Him. Remember His words to us in 1 John 4:4, *"He who is in you is greater than he who is in the world."* Although we are weak in ourselves, we are strong in Him and He wants us to say so:

> *Turn your shovels into swords, turn your hoes into spears.*
> *Let the weak one throw out his chest and say, "I'm tough, I'm a fighter."*
> *(Joel 3:10 TMSG)*

We are homesick for the Commander to arise in us and in others, so that we can be the warriors He desires and will use in the great end-time battles that are shaping up even now.

Another great spiritual weapon that we have is submission to God. *"Therefore submit to God. Resist the devil and he will flee from you"* (James 4:7).

God thinks very highly of those that submit to the Commander of Heaven's Armies as Malachi 3:16–4:3 states:

> Then those who feared the Lord spoke with each other, and the Lord listened to what they said. In his presence, a scroll of remembrance was written to record the names of those who feared him and always thought about the honor of his name.

> "They will be my people," says the Lord of Heaven's Armies. "On the day when I act in judgment, they will be my own special treasure. I will spare them as a father spares an obedient child. Then you will again see the difference between the righteous and the wicked, between those who serve God and those who do not."

> The Lord of Heaven's Armies says, "The day of judgment is coming, burning like a furnace. On that day the arrogant and the wicked will be burned up like straw. They will be consumed—roots, branches, and all.

> "But for you who fear my name, the Sun of Righteousness will rise with healing in his wings. And you will go free, leaping with joy like calves let out to pasture. On the day when I act, you will tread upon the wicked as

*if they were dust under your feet," says the
Lord of Heaven's Armies. (NLT)*

If you want to *"go free, leaping with joy like calves
let out to pasture,"* be the warrior you're called to be—
serve the Commander. For you were born for such a
time as this and you will not feel "at home" until you
fulfill your destiny. Your destiny at this time in history is
to play some part in the end-time battles. You may not
be on the "front lines" of the battle, but everyone has a
part to play. Therefore, as the battles grow more intense,
you will feel more and more homesick for the
Commander's orders—until you fulfill your destiny, your
purpose.

Homesick for the City

You are special to God. We are all special to God—so
much so that He gave His Son for each one of us. Even
so, there are those that God points out in Scripture as
especially pleasing to Him. One such person is
Abraham. Why did God point him out? Because he was
homesick. He was homesick for *the city* designed and
built by God.

> *Abraham was confidently looking forward
> to a city with eternal foundations, a city
> designed and built by God. (Hebrews 11:10
> NLT)*

Abraham died not having received the promised city
but still believed in it as his eternal home.

> *Each one of these people of faith died not yet having in hand what was promised, but still believing. How did they do it? They saw it way off in the distance, waved their greeting, and accepted the fact that they were transients in this world. People who live this way make it plain that they are looking for their true home. If they were homesick for the old country, they could have gone back any time they wanted. (Hebrews 11:13–15 TMSG)*

They were not homesick for the country they came from; they were homesick for *the city.*

> *But now they desire a better, that is, a heavenly country. Therefore God is not ashamed to be called their God, for He has prepared a city for them. (Hebrews 11:16)*

I am homesick for the city that comes down from heaven to the new earth God creates. This massive city has a length, width, and height of about 1,400 miles with a 216-foot high wall! God and His people will live in this city on the new earth. There will be no death, sadness, crying, or pain in this city. There will be no sun or moon because the glory of God is its light and the Lamb (Jesus) is its lamp. The city's gates will never be shut because there is no night there.

Wow! What a place to continue your growth in Christ—for I believe we will forever be growing in Him.

So who may enter this magnificent city? We find the answer in Revelation 21:27:

Nothing impure will ever enter it, nor will anyone who does what is shameful or deceitful, but only those whose names are written in the Lamb's book of life. (NIV)

If you want to increase your homesickness for this city, you can meditate on the last two chapters of the Bible—Revelation 21 and 22. You will find the details of the city I have written about in those two chapters.

I want to close this chapter with Revelation 22:17— the invitation to be a part of all of this:

And the Spirit and the bride say, "Come!" And let him who hears say, "Come!" And let him who thirsts come. Whoever desires, let him take the water of life freely.

Now What?

Father, You are my true home. I am homesick for Your face-to-face presence. Even so, You have not called me to heaven yet. Your calling for me now is on the earth. By Your Spirit, help me to bring all the homesickness to earth that I can. In the Commander's name I pray. Amen.

I'm homesick—
longing for your
salvation

Psalm 119:81 TMSG

Conclusion

O ne of the most familiar stories in the Bible is the birth of Jesus. Even many who are not Christians know the account of Jesus' birth. Told most often around Christmas time and celebrated throughout many parts of the world, it makes a fitting conclusion to this book. How? Because it parallels the "birth" of Jesus through us.

When others see Jesus coming forth out of us, the impact will be great since no one influences the earth more than Jesus Christ. When He is "conceived" and "birthed" in us, we too will have the greatest influence we can have on this earth.

God became human not to show us how to live as God, but to show us how we can live as human beings. His growth from His childhood to manhood is the blueprint for our growth. Even so, I am limiting this conclusion to the events in Luke chapter one.

In Luke 1:26–28 we see the first of the parallels with our growth in Christ.

> . . . *God sent the angel Gabriel to the Galilean village of Nazareth to a virgin engaged to be married to a man descended from David. His name was Joseph, and the virgin's name, Mary. Upon entering, Gabriel greeted her:*

Good morning!
You're beautiful with God's beauty,
Beautiful inside and out!
God be with you. (TMSG)

We did not choose to be "pregnant" with Jesus, He chose us. We are born again by His Spirit; it is totally God's work. He chose us to bear fruit—the fruit of the Spirit—the very nature of Jesus.

You didn't choose me, remember; I chose you, and put you in the world to bear fruit, fruit that won't spoil. As fruit bearers, whatever you ask the Father in relation to me, he gives you. (John 15:16 TMSG)

Here we also see a major element for our growth— how God views us. He sees us as *"beautiful with God's beauty, beautiful inside and out!"*

His love for us is the critical part of our foundation for growth in Christ—He sees us as **beautiful.** We must receive His perspective of us and cast down any thoughts contrary to His thoughts about us. This would be an excellent time to say it aloud, "I am beautiful!" "God says, 'I am beautiful inside and out!'"

You bless God the most by simply receiving His deep-never-changing love for you. He loves you the same on your best day as on your worst day. He loves it when you just enjoy Him as your loving Father. He is so excited about you and He wants you to receive His pleasure over you. He is pleased with you because you believe in His Son and all His Son did for you. Your faith is what pleases Him.

Some further parallels out of Luke chapter 1:

> What God thinks and says about you trumps anything anyone else thinks or says about you, so be in agreement with God. Nevertheless, it is normal to be quite shocked when you hear what God thinks about you just as Mary was (see verse 29).

> You have favor with God; you have nothing to fear. His grace is sufficient for you (see verse 30).

> In verses 31–33, we see that Jesus is God's greatest gift to the world and that we too are a gift to the world as God brings forth Jesus out of us.

> God choosing to reveal His Son through us is a great mystery. It will not come by human action as we see in verse 34.

> Jesus is brought forth in us by the Holy Spirit (see verse 35).

> There are others pregnant with God's promises. It does not matter how barren they have been (see verses 36–37).

God was inviting Mary to carry God Himself within her. We are being given this same invitation—*to carry the very heart of God!* This sounds incredible, but it is exactly what Jesus prayed the Father would do for us. ". . . that the love with which You loved Me may be in them . . ." (John 17:26).

254   Now What?

This book is full of invitations from God **to you,** now I conclude this book with what ought to be your invitation **to God**—which is the key to "conceiving" and "birthing" all God has called you to be in Christ (verse 38):

> *Then Mary said, "Behold the maidservant of the Lord! Let it be to me according to your word."*

I have included many Scriptures in this book so you can say with Mary, ***"Let it be to me according to your word."***

This is my closing prayer; let it be yours also.

Author Steven J. Campbell may be contacted
at his personal email:
stevecamp3@hotmail.com

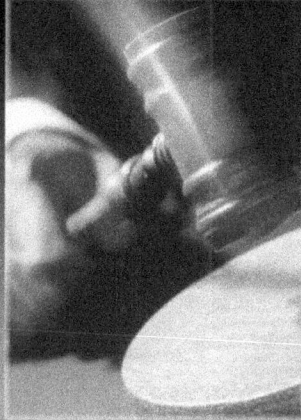

The Christian's Bill of Rights
A 31-Day Devotional to Help You Live Free

by Steven J. Campbell

*This book is for helping you live in hope
and the freedom that Jesus purchased for
you on the cross.*

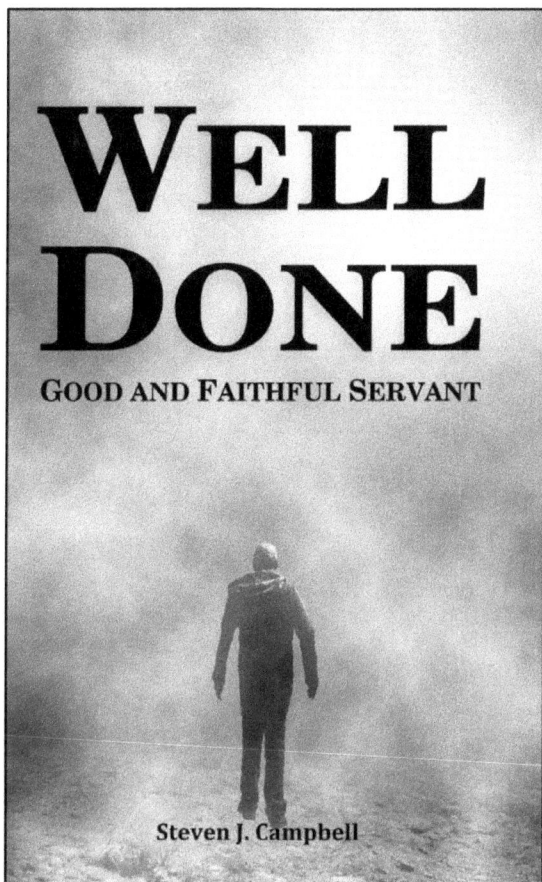

Well Done

Good and Faithful Servant

by Steven J. Campbell

This book is for helping you to fulfill your purpose in the great end-time harvest and to hear Jesus say to you, "Well done."

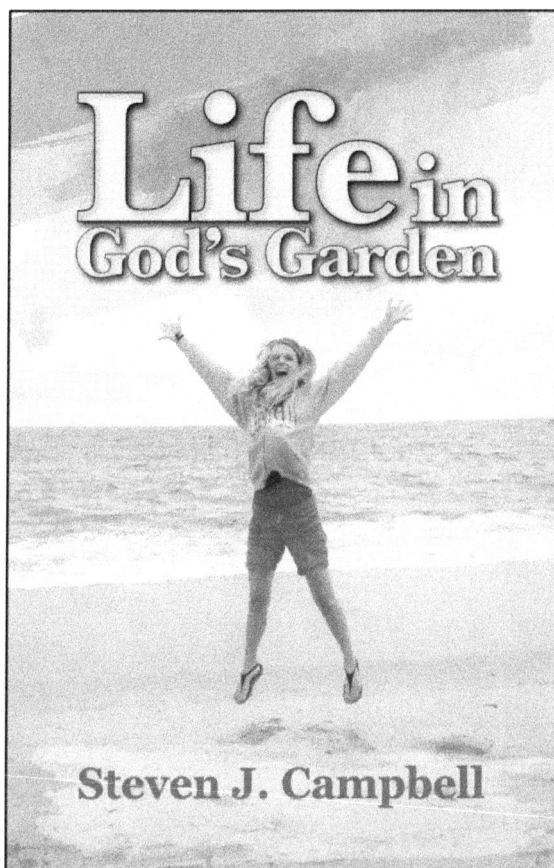

Life in God's Garden

by Steven J. Campbell
and
Austin J. Campbell

*This book is about how we are created to
live in a garden-type reality and
experience life in all its fullness.*

www.ingramcontent.com/pod-product-compliance
Lightning Source LLC
Chambersburg PA
CBHW060010050426
42448CB00012B/2691